D1461107

CLASSIC MOTORBIKES

Marks and Spencer p.l.c.
PO Box 3339
Chester CH99 9QS

shop online
www.marksandspencer.com

Copyright © Exclusive Editions 2008

All rights reserved. No part of this publication may be
reproduced, stored in a retrieval system, or transmitted
by any means, electronic, mechanical, photocopying,
recording or otherwise, without the prior permission of
the copyright holder.

ISBN 978-1-84805-417-2

Printed in China

The views expressed in this book are those of the author
but they are general views only and readers are urged to
consult a relevant and qualified specialist for individual
advice in particular situations. Marks and Spencer p.l.c.
and Exclusive Editions Ltd hereby exclude all liability to
the extent permitted by law for any errors or omissions in
this book and for any loss, damage or expense (whether
direct or indirect) suffered by a third party relying on any
information contained in this book.

Designed, produced and packaged by Stonecastle Graphics Ltd

Text by Roland Brown
Designed by Sue Pressley and Paul Turner
Edited by Anthony John

Photographic credits

Mac McDiarmid: page 28
Andrew Morland: pages 9 right, 10, 13, 21
Garry Stuart: pages 11, 12, 16, 17, 24, 38, 52, 83

Roland Brown library/www.motobike.net
    (fees to Riders for Health); photos by:
BMW: pages 14 above, 15, 75, 93 below
Honda: pages 77, 91

Photos © Roland Brown library/www.motobike.net by:
Roland Brown: pages 6, 7, 8, 9 left, 14 below, 54-55, 58,
    59 above, 70, 71, 72 above, 73, 74, 76, 80-81, 93 above
Jack Burnicle: pages 63, 66
Phil Masters: pages 4, 20, 22-23, 26, 27, 28-29, 30-31, 40, 41,
    42-43, 44, 45, 46-47, 48, 49, 53, 57, 60-61, 62, 72 below,
    79, 84, 85, 86-87, 88-89
Gold & Goose: pages 1, 56, 90, 92, 94-95
Mac McDiarmid: page 78
Oli Tennent: pages 3, 18-19, 25, 32-33, 34-35, 36-37, 39,
    59 below, 64-65, 67, 68-69, 82

Classic Motorbikes

A CELEBRATION OF THE WORLD'S GREATEST MOTORBIKES

Roland Brown

MARKS &
SPENCER

Contents

Introduction

The interest in classic motorcycles seems to grow with every passing year, as demonstrated by the huge variety of club runs, shows, races, auctions and other events taking place around the world. It's only natural for motorcyclists to admire the great machines of the past; those that were owned and cherished, or maybe just dreamed about, years ago, especially when many of these old bikes don't just look good, but are also great fun to ride.

In many cases they're also inexpensive to buy and run. Many enthusiasts still yearn for an immaculate Brough Superior or Ducati 750SS, but less exotic classics are much in demand too. While new models have been getting more powerful and sophisticated in recent years, a more important benefit to many motorcyclists has been the growing availability of older machines that are rideable, reliable and relatively cheap.

The precise nature of a classic bike has long been the subject of heated debate. Some machines built as recently as the 1980s generate as much nostalgia as an immaculate Indian Chief or BSA Gold Star does to an older generation. Many riders' formative motorcycling years were in the 1970s, when Japanese superbikes arrived, and glamorous Italian sportsters provided a thrilling alternative. Plenty of

Below: The world's first production motorcycle was the 1489cc Hildebrand & Wolfmüller, built in Germany for four years from 1894. The four-stroke parallel twin's cylinders lay horizontally. Maximum power output was 2.5hp, giving a top speed of almost 30mph (48km/h).

Opposite below: The progress in early motorcycle design is shown by two US-produced bikes: the steam-driven Geneva (left) from 1896; and the Thomas, which followed four years later with a 1.8hp petrol engine in its bicycle style frame.

other riders still affectionately recall the 1960s and earlier, when British bikes ruled the roads and Harley-Davidson, BMW and others joined in with their own distinctive machines.

From time to time people attempt to define a classic bike, in the way that veteran motorcycles are officially those built before 1915, and vintage covers those produced between 1915 and 1930. But it's rare that agreement is reached. Many very old bikes undoubtedly qualify, but a description or cut-off year is infinitely harder to pin down.

One dictionary definition of classic is 'of outstanding quality', and the machines selected for this book certainly fall into that category. Each is special in its own way; from Harley-Davidson's sophisticated 1915-model V-twin to Triumph's legendary Bonneville; from Honda's revolutionary CB750 four to Moto Guzzi's popular 250cc Airone. Together they show how the motorcycle has changed dramatically while its essential appeal has stayed much the same.

There are striking similarities between many machines of different eras. This book's first entry, FN's Four of more than a century ago, and the last, Ducati's 1989-model 851, share features ranging from a twistgrip throttle on the handlebars to the engine's location between the rider's shins. Between those two bikes are many unique, brilliant and very different machines. Whether with performance, technical innovation, commercial success or simply style, each played a part in bringing motorcycling to where it is today.

Above: The very first motorcycle was German engineer Gottlieb Daimler's 'Einspur' or 'One-track', a 264cc device with a wooden frame. It was ridden for roughly eight miles (13km) by Daimler's son Paul in 1885.

FN Four

Belgian firm FN's Four was one of the most successful machines of motorcycling's early years, as well as one of the most sophisticated. By no means everyone had been convinced by the relatively complex Four on its unveiling in 1904. French publication *France Automobile*'s reviewer commented that: 'It has a remarkable engine; however, we regard it more as a curiosity than a practical motor cycle'. But the Four would remain in production, through several redesigns, until 1926.

Its appeal was easy to understand. As well as the eye-catching four-cylinder engine that gave the bike its name, the Four incorporated advanced design features including telescopic forks and shaft final drive. Its smoothness and reliability gave it an advantage over most rival machines.

The FN initials were a shortening of Fabrique Nationale d'Armes de Guerre. The company from Herstal, near Liège, had been set up in 1899 to produce

Below: The FN Four was a well-produced machine with a tubular-steel frame, wide handlebars, efficient mudguards, bicycle-style saddle and, in the case of this immaculately restored example, a headlight plus a speedometer driven by the front wheel.

armaments. Bicycles had been added two years later, and in 1902 FN built its first motorcycles, using 225cc and 286cc single-cylinder engines. Those early singles prompted FN to attempt a more ambitious model, and to design it the company turned to Paul Kelecom, who had gained experience by designing and building engines under his own name. Kelecom's motors had been used by Ormonde, a London-based firm that had adopted one to compete in the prestigious Paris-Madrid marathon in 1903.

In an attempt to avoid the problems encountered in the Paris-Madrid, notably vibration and slipping drive belts, Kelecom set to work on a four-cylinder engine with shaft drive. The resultant 362cc powerplant's smoothness allowed it to be mounted in a relatively light, twin-loop frame. Other chassis details were thoughtfully designed, notably the telescopic front suspension system, which combined with a parallelogram linkage. No rear suspension or front brake were provided. Instead the FN featured two rear brakes: a drum that was operated by the rider pedalling backwards, and a hand-operated contracting band that worked on the outside of the drum.

That engine was the FN's main attraction. Valve layout was typical of the time, with cam-operated exhaust valves plus 'automatic' inlet valves – ie opened by piston suction alone, and closed by a light spring. Bottom-end design featured a long, one-piece crankshaft in a cast-iron crankcase whose four small mica windows allowed the rider to check that oil was reaching the main bearings.

Performance was smooth rather than spectacular, but by 1911 the Four's capacity had increased via 412cc to 491cc, giving a slightly increased top speed of about 40mph (64km/h). Another update raised capacity to 748cc just before World War I, during which the occupied FN factory at Herstal was used to build bikes for the Germany army.

Following the end of the War the Four's appeal faded. It was redesigned once again in 1923, this time gaining a chain final drive in place of the shaft. The Belgian firm finally ended its production three years later, but the classy Four had proved all its doubters wrong long before that.

Above: This Four's list of sophisticated features included footboards as well as the shaft final drive that was fitted to all but the last models.

Above left: The FN's engine size varied over the years. By the time this bike was built for the US market in 1908, capacity had increased from the original 362cc to 498cc.

FN Four (1906)

Engine Air-cooled inlet-over-exhaust eight-valve in-line four

Capacity 412cc (48 x 57mm)

Maximum power 4bhp

Transmission Single speed, shaft final drive

Frame Steel twin downtube

Suspension Telescopic front; rigid rear

Brakes None front; drum and contracting band rear

Weight 165lb (75kg) dry

Top speed 40mph (64km/h)

Zenith Gradua

Zenith motorcycles will long be remembered for the Gradua gear system, which was revolutionary when invented by the Surrey firm's designer Freddie Barnes in 1908. Until that time, the only way that the rider of a typical belt-drive motorcycle could adjust the machine's gearing was to alter the position of the crankshaft pulley that took drive from the engine to the rear wheel. This system's flaw was that if belt tension was correct in high gear, it was too slack in low gear.

Barnes' Gradua system got round that problem using a long handle, nicknamed the 'coffee grinder', which ran up the right side of the engine and was connected at its bottom to both the crankshaft pulley and the rear wheel. When the coffee-grinder was turned, it moved both the pulley and rear wheel spindle, maintaining drive-belt tension while the gearing was changed.

The Gradua was successfully fitted to various engines. Barnes himself rode a Zenith fitted with the device to win 53 hill climbs in 1911 alone, outclassing its single-speed rivals to such a degree that the organising Auto-Cycle Union barred the Gradua from entering further events.

Zenith utilised this ban to advertise their bikes, most memorably by introducing a badge that featured the word 'Barred' and pictured a motorcycle behind the bars of a jail. Zenith continued to use the logo long after the Gradua had been superseded by Rudge's Multi system. The firm eventually closed down in 1930, although small numbers were built by a London dealer into the 1940s.

Above: This 1914-model Zenith's 550cc JAP engine was one of many to benefit from the Gradua gear system.

Below: The Gradua's angled 'coffee-grinder' lever is visible above the petrol tank. The system would have helped this V-twin to carry the extra weight of a sidecar.

Pierce Four

The Pierce family of Buffalo, New York, was well known for bicycles and its glamorous Pierce-Arrow automobiles when Percy, son of founder George, set up the Pierce Cycle Company. Percy aimed to create a suitably upmarket two-wheeler, taking inspiration from the Belgian-built four-cylinder FN with which he had returned from a trip to Europe. His firm's debut machine became the first American-built four when it entered production in 1909.

FN's influence was clear in the Pierce's design, but the new bike was not a copy. Its larger, 696cc (43ci) engine was a side-valve design, complete with FN-style shaft drive. It produced about 4bhp. Sections of the frame were built from large-diameter steel tubes which also held fuel and oil. Quality of both workmanship and materials was outstandingly high, in keeping with the Pierce-Arrow reputation. The bike was advertised as the 'Pierce Vibrationless Motorcycle'; a machine that would 'give motorcar comfort, and travel comfortably from a mere walking pace up to the speed of the motorcar'.

The Four was certainly both smooth and fast, with a top speed of over 50mph (81km/h). It was also reliable enough to win several endurance events. Inevitably it was also expensive, with a price of $350 that made it the most costly machine on the US market in 1910. Unfortunately for Pierce, it was not profitable even at that price. An estimated 3500 of the sophisticated Fours had been sold by 1913, when the bankrupt Pierce Cycle Company built its last machine.

Above: The Pierce's cleverly engineered chassis used the large-diameter frame to hold fuel, and employed the final drive shaft as a structural component.

Above: The Pierce's smooth-running 696cc in-line four-cylinder engine used a side-valve layout to produce a maximum of 4bhp.

Cyclone

Cyclone's powerful and technically advanced V-twins were among the fastest and most spectacular bikes of their day, but not the most commercially successful. The Cyclone brand was launched in 1913 by the Joerns Motor Manufacturing Company, based in St Paul, Minnesota. Its machines were powered by 996cc V-twin engines with cylinders set at 45 degrees, and with the rarity of overhead camshafts, driven by bevel shaft.

Designer Andrew Stroud's powerplant was notable for its impressive power output – figures quoted range from 25bhp for the roadsters to 45bhp for the factory racebikes – and for its state-of-the-art engineering, which included lightweight conrods and a roller-bearing crankshaft. The chassis featured a steel frame that held the fuel tank between its horizontal top tubes, and cradled the engine in its U-shaped lower section. Most roadster models had leaf-spring suspension at both front and rear. Racebikes were generally unsprung and had distinctive yellow paintwork.

The Cyclones' speed and technology meant that they created quite a stir, boosted by the spectacular efforts of factory racer Don Johns. More publicity came when development engineer J A McNeil lapped the board track at Omaha, Nebraska at 111.1mph (178.8km/h) – beating existing US and world records so comprehensively that the suspicious authorities refused to ratify the achievement. But the Cyclones were as unreliable as they were fast, and frequently broke down in important races. Roadster sales were hit, the firm lacked finance for further development, and Cyclone folded in 1916 after just four eventful years of production.

Above: This 1915-model roadster combines Cyclone's yellow paintwork with left-spring front suspension, sprung saddle and a drum rear brake.

Above left: Its overhead camshafts with bevel-shaft drive helped make Cyclone's 45-degree V-twin engine one of the most powerful and sophisticated of its day.

Cyclone (1916)	
Engine	Air-cooled sohc four-valve 45-degree V-twin
Capacity	996cc
Maximum power	25bhp @ 5000rpm
Transmission	Chain final drive
Frame	Steel single downtube
Suspension	Leaf spring front & rear
Brakes	None front, drum rear
Weight	280lb (127kg)
Top speed	85mph (137km/h)

Harley-Davidson Model 11F

Harley-Davidson's Model 11F was not the only V-twin to make its mark for the Milwaukee factory in 1915. As well as the handsome and successful 989cc roadster, Harley built a tuned and lightened version called the Model 11K that brought the firm its first big racing success when rider Otto Walker won two prestigious long-distance events against factory opposition.

But it was the Model 11F roadster on which Harley's commercial success depended, and the 10bhp machine proved well up to the job. Six years after the Model D, the firm's first V-twin, had proved an unreliable disaster, the Model 11 showed that chief engineer William Harley and his three co-founders, the Davidson brothers, had learned much from that disappointment.

The 11F's V-twin engine kept the 45-degree cylinder angle that Harley had used all along, with inlet-over-exhaust valve layout, but it was a much improved machine. Its key features, some of which had been introduced over the previous few years, included a new frame with lower seat and sprung 'Ful Floteing' seatpost, plus footboards, enclosed valve springs, kick-starter, a more sophisticated lubrication system, and two-speed transmission with optional chain instead of belt final drive.

The Model 11F had a top speed of 60mph (97km/h), handled well with the help of girder fork front suspension, and enhanced Harley's reputation for strength and reliability. Its basic design would be retained, through numerous updates, for another 15 years as the Milwaukee firm confirmed its status as one of America's leading manufacturers.

Above: The Model 11F featured the grey paintwork of many early Harleys but was a much more sophisticated bike than the firm's first V-twin of 1909.

Above: Harley's 45-degree degree V-twin gained a three-speed gearbox in 1915, but starting remained by pedal until a kickstarter was introduced for the following year.

BMW R32

The Bayerische Motoren Werke, which had built BMW aircraft engines during World War I, was one of many German firms that turned to motorcycle manufacture in the early 1920s, when forced to abandon aircraft work under the Treaty of Versailles. The company had employed more than 3500 people during the War, having been formed in 1917 following an alliance of two leading aircraft engine manufacturers, Otto and Rapp.

The first BMW bike was a simple motorised bicycle called the Flink. It was powered by a proprietary Kurier 148cc two-stroke engine, and was not a success. In 1921, BMW engineer Martin Stolle designed a 494cc flat-twin side-valve engine, designated the M2B15, which the Munich firm sold to other manufacturers including Victoria, Heller and Bison. The M2B15 produced 6bhp and was designed to be mounted with its cylinders running in line with the bike.

A year later the R32 was created by Max Friz, an aeroplane engineer who was one of BMW's original directors. Friz designed a new flat-twin engine that retained the 494cc capacity, but sat at 90 degrees to the previous unit, with cylinders across the frame, giving improved cooling. The engine incorporated a three-speed

Above: BMW established the transverse flat-twin layout with the firm's very first bike.

Above: The R32's drive shaft design prevented rear wheel suspension, but the twin's front end benefited from a leaf-spring system.

BMW R32 (1923)

Engine Air-cooled ohv pushrod four-valve flat-twin

Capacity 494cc (68 x 68mm)

Maximum power 8.5hp @ 3200rpm

Transmission Three-speed, shaft final drive

Frame Steel twin tube

Suspension Leaf spring front; rigid rear

Brakes Drum front; rim rear

Weight 269lb (122kg)

Top speed 55mph (88km/h)

Opposite: Large mudguards and the upturned alloy footboards helped make the first BMW an impressively clean and practical machine.

gearbox, worked by a lever to the right of the fuel tank, and shaft final drive. A steel mushroom was fitted to the top of each cylinder head to give protection in the event of a crash.

The chassis was based on a triangulated, twin-downtube steel frame. Front suspension was by a similar system to that used by Indian; a variation of the leaf-spring design that incorporated trailing links plus slim rods running up to forward-projecting laminated springs. The shaft drive meant that no rear suspension could be used so a sprung saddle was employed to provide a comfortable ride. Braking was provided by a drum on the front wheel, plus a friction device working on a dummy wheel rim at the rear.

The R32 motor produced 8.5bhp, good for a top speed of about 55mph (88km/h), and the bike was neatly finished and well built, with electric lighting and enclosed valve gear. The BMW generated great excitement when unveiled at the Paris Motorcycle Salon in 1923. Most machines of the day were assembled using parts from various sources but the R32 stood out for having clearly been designed as a complete entity. Its alloy footboards were neatly integrated with the engine and frame. The footboards' raised fronts combined with the large mudguards and the shaft final drive system to make the BMW a notably clean and practical machine.

Although expensive, the R32 was a success. More than 3000 units were sold during the next four years, establishing BMW as a serious motorcycle manufacturer. The model was developed by engineer Rudolf Schleicher to create the R37, which had an overhead-valve instead of side-valve layout, and produced a considerably increased maximum of 16bhp. Schleicher and others rode the R37 in variety of competitive events. Production of the R32 ended in 1926, but its real legacy is that well into the next century, BMW was still building bikes powered by air-cooled boxer engines.

Indian Powerplus

L egendary long-distance ace Erwin 'Cannonball' Baker gave Indian's
Powerplus the perfect introduction following the bike's unveiling in 1915.
Baker rode for 3 days, 9 hours and 15 minutes to break the record for the
1655.5-mile (2663.7km) Three Flags route from Canada to Mexico, gaining much
publicity for the Springfield firm's new 998cc V-twin.

The Powerplus proved a big success when it was launched to the public in the
following year. Designer Charles Gustafson Snr's creation retained the 42-degree
cylinder that Indian had established for its V-twins, and replaced the previous
F-head (or inlet-over-exhaust) valve layout for a superior side-valve design that
increased output to a claimed 18bhp.

That extra power gave the Powerplus a top speed of over 60mph (97km/h).
The new motor was also cleaner and quieter, due to its enclosed valve gear. It had
a three-speed gearbox with a hand change and foot clutch. There was also a back-
up hand clutch, on the right handlebar because Indian's throttle was on the left.
Leaf-spring front suspension was fitted as standard, with a leaf-spring available as
an option at the rear too.

The Indian's resultant comfort was appreciated by riders including Cannonball
Baker, who also rode the Powerplus to set 24-hour records both overland in
Australia and on the board track at Cincinnati, where he covered over 1500 miles
(2413km) in a day. The dependable Powerplus remained in Indian's range until
1924, although for the last two years it was called the Standard to prevent it
overshadowing Indian's newer Chief V-twin.

*Above: The Powerplus was a fast and refined
machine by 1918 standards, featuring lights, leaf-
spring suspension front and rear, plus enclosed
valve gear for its 42-degree V-twin engine.*

Indian Powerplus (1918)

Engine Air-cooled four-valve side-valve
42-degree V-twin

Capacity 988cc (79.4 x 100.8mm)

Maximum power 18bhp

Transmission Three-speed, chain final drive

Frame Steel single downtube

Suspension Leaf-spring front & (optional) rear

Brakes None front; drum rear

Weight 410lb (186kg)

Top speed 65mph (105km/h)

Excelsior Super X

Excelsior's V-twins were among the world's best bikes in the last century's second decade. The Chicago firm's sophisticated roadsters were built in motorcycling's largest factory, and evaluated on its rooftop test track. Excelsior's rapid racebikes regularly beat their rivals from the Harley-Davidson and Indian firms that were fellow members of American motorcycling's unofficial 'Big Three' manufacturers.

Like Harley, Excelsior favoured a 45-degree cylinder angle for its V-twin roadsters, which began in 1908 with an 820cc model. A 992cc bike followed three years later, and by 1918 the engine with its F-head (or inlet-over-exhaust) valve layout produced about 20bhp. By this time Excelsior had introduced a three-speed gearbox and foot clutch, alongside features including leaf-spring front suspension, footboards and a sprung saddle.

The Excelsior ran well, with a top speed of about 80mph (130km/h). The firm had agreed with other American manufacturers to halt racing during World War I, but the high-speed exploits of Excelsior rider Wells Bennett provided some welcome publicity. In 1918 Bennett covered the 300-mile (483km) desert route from Los Angeles to Needles in California at an average of 42.3mph (68km/h).

Excelsior began a trend in 1925 by launching the 750cc (45 cubic inch) Super X, which triggered the growth of 750cc Class C racing. But although Excelsior restyled the Super X to good effect in 1929, the V-twin could not turn round the firm's financial problems, which worsened in the Depression shortly afterwards. In 1931, owner Ignaz Schwinn dramatically abandoned motorcycle production. The famous Excelsior marque was no more.

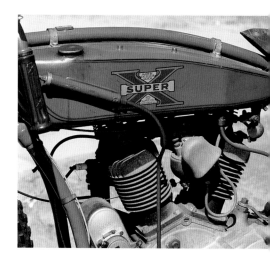

Above: The Super X's 750cc or 45 cubic inch engine capacity set a trend, and inspired the competitive Class C racing division.

Below: The rider of this Super X racer had no brakes to worry about, but did have to remember to give the engine some oil with the tank-mounted pump.

Brough Superior

The mighty V-twins from George Brough's Nottingham workshop were the most glamorous and exotic motorcycles of the 1920s and '30s. In their maker's own words, the Brough Superior was a 'big solo machine, made up to an ideal and not down to a price'. The bikes certainly had the performance to match their high price.

Brough combined his own frames with V-twin powerplants from JAP and Matchless to create innovative, fast and expensive roadburners. Bought-in components were not only the best available, but in many cases had to be improved still further before being accepted for Brough use.

George Brough was a fine rider as well as engineer, and won many races, sprints and hill climbs, as did other notable 'Brufsup' riders including Eric Fernihough, Freddie Dixon and Bert Le Vack. He also excelled in marketing and was not notably modest, highlighted when he named his machine the Superior – to the annoyance of his father, a manufacturer of flat-twin bikes himself, who retorted: 'I suppose that makes mine the Brough Inferior?'

The 1924 Brough Superior catalogue stated that: 'It is very satisfying to know that you are astride a machine which, if you wish, can leave behind anything on wheels.' That was a bold claim, as were others such as 'It is actually possible to ride hands off at 60mph', and 'It starts first kick from stone cold'. But if anyone could justify such statements it was Brough, who used the line 'the Rolls-Royce of Motorcycles' in his advertising, and was allowed to continue after a displeased

Above: Broughs' exotic nature and high-quality construction justified the firm's advertising boast: 'the Rolls-Royce of motorcycles'.

Below: A big chromed fuel tank was almost as much of a distinctive Brough Superior feature as the V-twin engine.

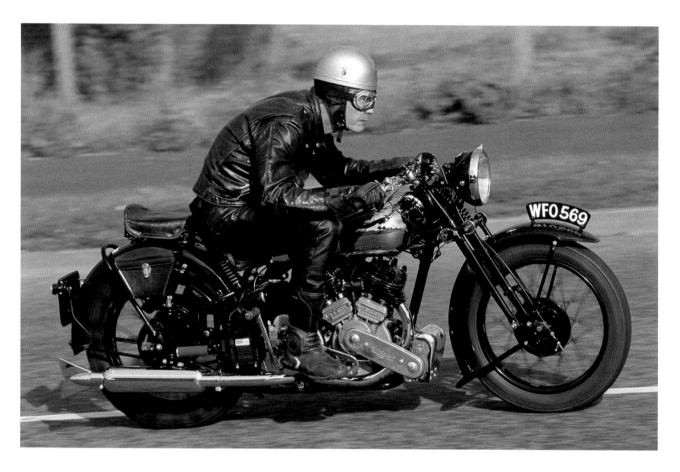

Above: *Brough's use of premium quality cycle parts gave the Superior excellent handling and 'hands-off' stability at speed.*

Rolls executive had arrived at the Nottingham workshop to find show bikes being assembled by workers wearing white gloves.

Approximately 3000 Superiors were produced during Brough's two decades in business. Many of those were the SS80, named after its 80mph (128km/h) top speed. It used a side-valve V-twin engine, latterly a 990cc, 50-degree Matchless powerplant that incorporated numerous modifications from the units fitted to the Matchless Model X. As well as obvious features such as the Brough Superior name on the tappet and timing covers, the SS80 had modified cylinder porting and a different exhaust system.

Brough's more powerful, overhead-valve SS100 was initially powered by a 980cc, 45bhp JAP engine, and was delivered with a signed guarantee that the bike had been timed at over 100mph (161km/h) for a quarter of a mile. Fewer than 400 were built. Even more special versions included the SS100 Alpine Grand Sports, built for fast touring, and the racing Pendine, with high-compression engine and guaranteed 110mph (176km/h) top speed.

Brough continually updated the Superior's specification, introducing optional rear suspension in 1928, foot gear change in 1935 and a four-speed Norton gearbox a year later. His many innovations included flyscreens, twin headlamps, crashbars and panniers. T E Shaw, alias 'Lawrence of Arabia', was a devoted Brough enthusiast – and sadly one of the least fortunate. Lawrence, who owned a special stainless-steel petrol tank which he fitted to his series of Superiors, died in 1935 after crashing his SS100.

Brough Superior SS80 (1937)

Engine Air-cooled side-valve four-valve 50-degree V-twin

Capacity 990cc (84 x 90mm)

Maximum power 35bhp @ 4000rpm

Transmission Four-speed, chain final drive

Frame Steel single downtube

Suspension Girder forks; plunger rear

Brakes Drum front & rear

Weight 420lb (191kg)

Top speed 80mph (129km/h)

Scott Flying Squirrel

'Silence, performance, simplicity and smoothness give the Scott an individuality which cannot be rivalled by any other make of machine.' the Flying Squirrel's brochure enthused in the 1940s, with little fear of contradiction. The Yorkshire firm's 596cc, liquid-cooled two-stroke parallel twin was unlike any other bike, continuing a tradition of innovative engineering that stretched back to the machines with which founder Alfred Angas Scott had started production back in 1904.

The Flying Squirrel was launched in 1926, three years after Scott's death. It featured a conventional petrol tank and frame, in place of previous models' cylindrical tanks and open frames. The firm's trademark engine format was retained, in 498 and 596cc capacities. The larger model produced 25bhp, giving a 70mph (112km/h) top speed with impressive smoothness and a unique high-pitched 'yowl' from the exhaust.

After World War II Scott briefly resumed production of the rigid framed Flying Squirrel, updated from girder to telescopic forks. But the bikes were heavy and underpowered, the 596cc engine having barely been updated since gaining detachable cylinder heads in 1934. The Squirrel was also expensive and not particularly reliable, and few were sold.

In 1950, struggling Scott was bought by Birmingham-based enthusiast Matt Holder. He added a swing-arm frame and continued developing and selling Squirrels in tiny numbers right up until 1978. The Squirrel's remarkable production life of more than half a century highlighted the advanced design and unique appeal of the original machine.

Above: The softly-tuned Flying Squirrel had a much more solid, touring feel than the Yorkshire firm's sportier early models, and needed its engine flexibility because the gearbox had only three speeds.

Below: The Flying Squirrel retained Scott's traditional two-stroke parallel twin engine layout, but had a conventional fuel tank and frame instead of the old bike's cylindrical tank and open frame.

Norton CS1

The CS1 was perhaps the most significant of the great single-cylinder Nortons of the 1920s and '30s. The Birmingham firm's side-valve and pushrod-operated bikes had already scored many race wins at the Isle of Man TT and elsewhere. But it was the CS1, with its overhead camshaft valve operation, that reignited the marque following its launch in 1927.

At that time Norton was struggling, following the death two years earlier of founder James Lansdowne 'Pa' Norton, following long-standing heart problems. The firm's ageing pushrod single engine was becoming less competitive. It was redesigned with an overhead cam by Walter Moore, Norton's talented development engineer and race team boss.

Moore's 490cc CS1 (Cam Shaft 1) engine retained traditional long-stroke dimensions of 79 x 100mm, and replaced the pushrods with an overhead cam, driven via a shaft running in a vertical tower. It produced 20bhp and was an immediate success when introduced in 1927. Norton's Alec Bennett won that year's Senior TT, and Stanley Woods broke the lap record on a similar machine. The following year the CS1 was offered as a sporting roadster.

Norton was rocked when Moore quit to join Germany's NSU, whose later 500SS resembled the CS1 so closely that Norton workers claimed NSU stood for 'Norton Spares Used'. In 1931 Norton's Arthur Carroll redesigned the single's camshaft drive, switching the exhaust pipe from the left side to the right. Norton dominated the 1932 Senior TT, and the following year released a roadgoing version, the International, that remained successful for the rest of the decade.

Above: The CS1's highlight was its 490cc engine's overhead camshaft, driven by the bevel shaft that ran down the right side of the cylinder.

Above: The silver-tanked CS1's exhaust pipe exited to the left, which made the single easily distinguishable from the later International with its right-sided pipe.

Triumph Speed Twin

The Speed Twin changed the face of motorcycling in a way that only a handful of bikes have done. Triumph chief engineer Edward Turner's 498cc parallel twin was launched into a world of mostly single-cylinder machines in 1937. Its immediate popularity gave Triumph a huge and lasting boost, and resulted in rival British manufacturers basing their ranges on the parallel-twin engine for the next three decades.

One short blast on the Speed Twin was usually all a rider needed to appreciate the benefits of a quick, torquey machine that was notably smoother than comparable singles. It was also lighter than Triumph's own Tiger 90 single, and barely more expensive. And Turner's legendary eye for style ensured that the maroon-and-chrome machine looked the part too. Given all that, it's no surprise that the Speed Twin and its descendants dominated the post-War motorcycling scene.

The key to the Speed Twin's success was that sweet-running vertical twin engine. Twin camshafts, driven by gear from the crankshaft, operated pushrods with tubes set into the vees between the cylinders at the front and rear. The

Triumph Speed Twin (1938)	
Engine Air-cooled ohv four-valve pushrod parallel twin	
Capacity 498cc (63 x 80mm)	
Maximum power 29bhp @ 6000rpm	
Transmission Four-speed, chain final drive	
Frame Steel twin downtube	
Suspension Girder front; rigid rear	
Brakes Drum front & rear	
Weight 365lb (166kg)	
Top speed 95mph (153km/h)	

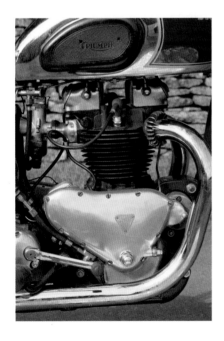

Above: The Speed Twin's powerful, compact and reasonably smooth-running 498cc engine triggered the parallel-twin revolution that transformed motorcycling in the 1940s.

Right: This 1946-model Speed Twin features the telescopic forks that replaced the original girders when Triumph restarted production after the War. Other changes included a larger fuel tank, magneto ignition and restyled headlight.

Below: With its lean and attractive lines, enhanced by a touch of chrome, the Speed Twin demonstrated Triumph design chief Edward Turner's famed eye for style.

engine was not in a particularly high state of tune, which helped make it pleasantly smooth-running, but still produced a very respectable peak output of 29bhp at 6000rpm.

From the moment the Speed Twin was launched, its engine was much praised for its flexibility, which allowed the bike to pull from below 30mph (48km/h) in top gear, and even trickle along at slower speed in top without complaint. The Triumph was fast, too. The 1937 model was tested by *The Motor Cycle* at 107mph (172km/h) – 'truly an amazing figure for a fully equipped 500' – although 95mph (153km/h) was a more typical figure.

Another important feature of the motor was its compact size, which allowed it to be fitted into the Tiger 90's single-downtube frame, without altering the line of the drive chain. As well as reducing Triumph's development costs, that helped ensure the twin's acceptance in the conservative two-wheeled world of the late 1930s and '40s. The chassis gave good handling, although the unsprung rear end had a tendency to bounce over bumps at speed. The front and rear drum brakes were very efficient.

The Speed Twin was an immediate hit, and in 1939 was joined in the range by the tuned Tiger 100, named in typically shrewd Turner fashion after its 100mph (161km/h) top speed. The War soon put paid to Triumph's production of civilian machines, but both models were revived in 1946. For its comeback the Speed Twin was fitted with telescopic forks instead of the original girders; a larger, four-gallon petrol tank; and magneto ignition (instead of the original magdyno) with a dynamo to power the restyled headlight.

Both the Speed Twin and Tiger 100 would remain hugely successful throughout the 1940s, being joined in 1950 by the Thunderbird, with its torquier 650cc engine. By this time most other British manufacturers had joined in by developing parallel twins of their own. The Speed Twin and its descendants had shown the way forward.

Indian Scout

The middleweight Scout was a long-running success for Indian, confirming designer Charles B Franklin's belief that many American riders would appreciate a smaller V-twin than the firm's 998cc Powerplus, from which it was descended. The original Scout, launched in 1919, had a 615cc (37 cubic inch) side-valve engine in Indian's familiar 42-degree layout. It produced 11bhp, was capable of 60mph (97km/h), handled better than the Powerplus and soon gained a reputation for reliability.

An important Scout development came in 1927 when its engine was enlarged to 750cc (45ci) to compete with Excelsior's Super X. The following year's 101 Scout combined a long wheelbase and low seating position to deliver outstanding handling, and became very popular. Its 22bhp engine gave a top speed of 75mph (121km/h), and its reliability justified the Indian advertising line: 'You can't wear out an Indian Scout'. Other innovations included a drum front brake, plus new carburettor and oil pump designs.

Numerous Scout variants were introduced over the years, not all with good results. The Standard Scout of 1932 was heavy; the 500cc Scout Pony lacked power. Indian had more joy in 1934 with the Sport Scout, which retained the traditional 750cc capacity and combined lively performance with agile handling. It responded well to tuning and was ridden successfully in TT events, hill climbs and Class C dirt-track races. In 1940, Indian fitted the Sport Scout with big 'skirted' mudguards. Production ended two years later but stripped-down Scouts were still winning races in the 1950s.

Above: This 1931 Scout features leaf-spring front suspension, hard-tail rear and a 750cc V-twin engine with 42-degree cylinder angle.

Indian Sport Scout (1934)

Engine Air-cooled four-valve side-valve 42-degree V-twin

Capacity 744cc (73 x 89mm)

Maximum power 22bhp

Transmission Three-speed, chain final drive

Frame Steel twin downtube

Suspension Girder front; none rear

Brakes Drum front & rear

Weight 450lb (204kg)

Top speed 80mph (129km/h)

Sunbeam S8

The S8 was an attempt to go back to basics for Sunbeam, following the mechanical problems and poor sales of its controversial predecessor the S7. When the S8 was launched in 1949, its traditional black paintwork, slim look, conventional telescopic forks and narrow tyres were all in contrast to the bulkier S7, which had arrived two years earlier with unusual mist-green paintwork, innovative front forks and huge balloon tyres.

At heart the S8 was very similar to its imaginative but flawed forebear, for it shared the S7's 487cc tandem twin-cylinder engine layout and twin-downtube frame design. But the powerplant used higher compression ratio and a freer-breathing exhaust to increase peak output slightly to 26bhp, and more importantly was made more reliable by modifications including new pistons and extra oil capacity. And the chassis was improved by its use of BSA forks in place of the S7's undamped and poor-performing units, plus a revised rubber-mounting system that more efficiently isolated the twin-cylinder unit's vibration.

Performance was more lively than that of the S7. At 400lb (182kg) the S8 was substantially lighter, and it accelerated enthusiastically towards a top speed of just over 80mph (130km/h). The newer model handled better, too, and its engine proved reliable as well as smooth and easy to start. The S8 was also cheaper than the uprated S7 De Luxe that was introduced at the same time. But although the S8 sold reasonably well, all Sunbeam production was stopped following parent company BSA's merger with Triumph in 1956.

Sunbeam S8 (1949)	
Engine	Air-cooled sohc four-valve tandem twin
Capacity	487cc (70 x 63.5mm)
Maximum power	26bhp @ 5800rpm
Transmission	Four-speed, shaft final drive
Frame	Steel twin downtube
Suspension	Telescopic front; plunger rear
Brakes	Drum front & rear
Weight	400lb (182kg)
Top speed	82mph (132km/h)

Below: The S8's tandem twin powerplant was the S7's 487cc unit, strengthened and tuned with a higher compression ratio and a less restrictive exhaust system.

Left: The S8 was a much more conventional looking bike than the S7, and its reduced weight helped both acceleration and handling.

Gilera Saturno

G ilera's greatest bikes of the 1950s were the mighty four-cylinder racers that won six 500cc world championships, but the Italian factory's outstanding roadsters were more simple singles of similar capacity. The best known of those was the Saturno, which was launched in 1946 and remained popular through the following decade due to its combination of style, agility, reliability and lively performance.

The Saturno was designed by Giuseppe Salmaggi, and was a development of the so-called 'eight-bolt' (Otto Bulloni) single that had been Gilera's main 500cc machine in the late 1930s. The 499cc engine had pushrod-operated valves closed by hairpin springs, and a four-speed gearbox. Two roadgoing versions were built. The Sport had an aluminium cylinder head, produced 22bhp and was good for 85mph (137km/h). The Touring model was in a lower state of tune and used a cast-iron cylinder head.

Early Saturnos had girder forks and Gilera's own brand of rear suspension: horizontal springs in tubes, with friction dampers. Telescopic forks and vertical shocks were introduced in the early 1950s. The bike became popular thanks to its excellent roadgoing performance and some impressive racing results, the first of which was Carlo Bandirola's win at the Sanremo circuit in 1947, which led to the Saturno racer being known as the Sanremo.

Saturnos were not competitive at Grand Prix level but were raced successfully in Italy throughout the 1950s. Production ended in 1959, after sales of the single had been hit by the introduction of the similarly priced Fiat 500 car.

Above: With its lean lines and Italian racing red paintwork the Saturno Sport was a very stylish machine. This bike dates from 1950, two years before Gilera updated the single with telescopic forks and twin shocks.

Gilera Saturno Sport (1950)	
Engine Air-cooled ohv 2-valve pushrod single	
Capacity 499cc (84 x 90mm)	
Maximum power 22hp @ 5000rpm	
Transmission Four-speed, chain final drive	
Frame Steel single downtube	
Suspension Girder front; horizontal springs rear	
Brakes Drum front & rear	
Weight 385lb (175kg)	
Top speed (road trim) 85mph (137km/h)	

Moto Guzzi Airone

Moto Guzzi's little 250cc Airone was one of the most popular Italian roadsters of the 1940s and early '50s – a golden era for Guzzi, when the firm's horizontal single-cylinder racebikes won a string of 250 and 350cc world championships. That engine layout had characterised the Mandello marque ever since Carlo Guzzi and his friend Giorgio Parodi had built their the first machines, the 'GP' or Guzzi-Parodi racer of 1920 and the roadgoing Normale that had followed.

The Airone – Heron in English – was launched in 1939, based on a roadster called the 250 PE. The pushrod-operated single produced a claimed 9.5bhp, giving a top speed of 60mph (97km/h). The bike weighed just 297lb (135kg) and was well equipped, featuring telescopic forks and large mudguards, plus legshields as standard equipment.

There was one Airone model until 1949, when the Airone Sport was introduced, featuring a hotted-up engine with new camshaft, bigger carburettor and higher compression ratio. The Sport produced 13.5bhp at 6000rpm, a 4bhp increase on the standard model, which became the Turismo. The Sport cornered and stopped well thanks to a new chassis incorporating a tubular rather than pressed-steel frame, plus 19-inch Borrani wheels and larger drum brakes.

Guzzi modified the single several times, notably by uprating the Turismo with more power and the Sport's tubular-steel frame. But those changes couldn't maintain the Airone's popularity in the mid-1950s, in the face of opposition from 125 and 175cc models that offered similar or better performance at a lower price. Production eventually ended in 1957.

Above: *The Airone's 250cc engine was one of the smaller examples of Guzzi's trademark flat single, and like the other versions incorporated an external 'bacon slicer' flywheel.*

Below: *This stylish Airone Sport was built in 1951, the year that Bruno Ruffo won his second 250cc world championship on Guzzi's 'Gambalunghino' (Little long-leg) single.*

Vincent Rapide

Vincent's thundering V-twins were the world's fastest and finest roadsters in the 1940s and early '50s, combining exhilarating high performance with stable handling, excellent braking and long-distance cruising ability. The machines created at Vincent's base at Stevenage in Hertfordshire were also stylish, well built and inevitably expensive.

Philip Vincent had started his motorcycle operation in 1928 after buying the defunct HRD marque. Engines from JAP, Villiers and Rudge were fitted until 1934 when Vincent and his Australian chief engineer Phil Irving produced the firm's own unit, a 500cc 'high cam' single, which was used to power the sporty Comet and touring Meteor.

Irving designed Vincent's first V-twin in 1936 by combining two Comet cylinders at 47 degrees. The resultant 998cc Rapide produced 45bhp and was capable of an impressive 110mph (177km/h), although its power led to transmission problems.

Below: This Series C Rapide, produced in 1950, featured Vincent's Girdraulic front forks instead of the previous Series B model's Brampton girders.

It was nicknamed the 'Snarling Beast', and also the 'Plumber's Nightmare' due to its mass of external oil lines.

Following World War II, Vincent introduced the Series B Rapide, powered by a new engine with cylinders at 50 degrees, and unit-construction engine and gearbox. The engine formed a stressed member of the chassis, so no frame downtubes were required. The Rapide was a superb machine, its blend of power plus fine handling from its more compact chassis giving performance that no other roadster could match.

The tester from *Motor Cycle* wrote of the Rapide in 1947 that: 'there has never been a production model with so much to commend it as a road-burner's dream. From 40mph up to the maximum of over 100mph there is thrilling performance available at the twist of the grip… Though the big engine and high gearing suggest easy, loping, fussless mile-eating, there is searing acceleration available if required. Standing start getaways against the watch provide a memorable thrill and leave a black line of rubber on the road surface.'

The Series C Rapide followed in 1948, featuring Vincent's Girdraulic forks in place of the previous Brampton girders. A hydraulic damping unit was added between the diagonally mounted, side-by-side rear shock units, to assist the original friction dampers. The Rapide's thick dual-seat and efficient suspension made the bike comfortable on the long, high-speed trips that were its speciality.

Even faster was the tuned Black Shadow, whose 55bhp black-finished engine gave a top speed of over 120mph (192km/h), recorded on a large Smith's speedometer calibrated to 150mph (241km/h). American ace Rollie Free famously reached that speed on Vincent's race-specification Black Lightning, after stripping to swimming trunks and shoes to set a world record for unsupercharged bikes at just over 150.313mph (241.85km/h). Other legendary Vincents include Gunga Din, Nero and the supercharged Super Nero ridden by George Brown.

Vincent's enduring problem was that the bikes were unprofitable, despite their high prices. In 1955 the firm introduced Series D models, the Black Knight and tuned Black Prince, but the public was not yet ready for their futuristic, all-enveloping bodywork. Sales were slow, and Vincent abandoned production before the end of that year.

Above: The Rapide was a magnificently fast and long-legged roadburner that was happy cruising at high speed for long distances, and had the stability to match.

Vincent Rapide Series C (1949)	
Engine	Air-cooled ohv four-valve 50-degree V-twin
Capacity	998cc (84 x 90mm)
Maximum power	45bhp @ 5300rpm
Transmission	Four-speed, chain final drive
Frame	Steel spine
Suspension	Girder front; twin shocks rear
Brakes	Twin drums front & rear
Weight	455lb (207kg)
Top speed	110mph (177km/h)

Left: With its black paintwork, purposeful look and big V-twin engine the Rapide was a stylish and tidy looking machine that had long ago lost its 'Plumber's Nightmare' nickname.

Ariel Square Four

Ariel's Square Four retained its name and distinctive engine layout through its long production life, during which it was repeatedly updated from the original 497cc model of 1931 to the 997cc 4G MkII of 1958. Throughout that 27-year period, which saw a doubling of engine capacity and a huge increase in performance, the Square Four maintained its assets of four-cylinder power and smoothness with compact size. Unfortunately for Ariel, the model's disadvantages – high production costs and the problems of cooling the sheltered rear cylinders – also remained.

The Square Four was the brainchild of young design genius Edward Turner, who showed several factories sketches of his new engine – essentially two pairs of parallel twins, with crankshafts geared together – before Ariel boss Jack Sangster gave him the go-ahead. The resultant powerplant ran very smoothly, and was so compact that it fitted into a frame almost identical to that of Ariel's 500cc single.

That first Square Four was enthusiastically received when unveiled at London's Olympia Show in 1930. It featured a chain-driven overhead camshaft and exhaust manifolds integral with the cylinder head, so only two pipes emerged from the engine. Turner's original design had used an integral three-speed gearbox, but the production bike used a four-speed box, with hand change.

Above: The Square Four 4G's 997cc engine produced 34bhp and was heavily finned in an attempt to cool the rear cylinders.

Below: This 1952-model 'Squariel' was a stylish bike whose flexible engine's performance justified the firm's boast of 'Ten to a hundred in top gear'.

For 1932 the engine was enlarged to 597cc, the smaller engine being dropped shortly afterwards. In this form the Square Four produced 24bhp at 6000rpm, and stayed smooth to its top speed of 85mph (136km/h). Despite its high price the 'Squariel' was popular, especially with sidecar enthusiasts. But its flywheels were too light, and cylinder head cooling was a problem.

Turner left for Triumph, and for 1937 Ariel's new chief engineer Val Page designed revised 597cc and 997cc models, the 4F and 4G. They featured longer-stroke dimensions, pushrod valve operation, and extra cylinder head finning plus a tunnel between the cylinders, to allow cooling air to the rear cylinders. A Solex carburettor, placed conventionally behind the motor, replaced the previous forward-mounted Amal. The larger 4G produced 34bhp and was very flexible, prompting Ariel's famous advertising line: 'Ten to a hundred in top gear'. But reliability problems lingered.

Ariel reduced weight and improved cooling after World War II with a new all-aluminium engine, and in 1953 introduced the comprehensively revised Square Four 4G MkII. This was a stylish bike that emphasised its engine layout with four separate exhaust downpipes for the first time. Even in this final form the engine was prone to overheat in traffic, but the impressively broad power delivery allowed the rider to enjoy the bike's smooth cruising ability with little need to use the four-speed gearbox.

By now the Ariel had adopted telescopic forks and plunger rear suspension, but the Square Four's handling did not match the performance of its engine. Even so, the 4G MkII was a notably smooth and luxurious machine. Production finally ended in 1958, when Ariel abandoned four-strokes to build the Leader two-stroke. The Square Four's reputation as a high-class tourer lives on.

Above: *The later Square Four 4G MkII announced its four-cylinder engine layout with a quartet of exhaust downpipes. This 1959-model bike was one of the last to be built before Ariel abandoned four-stroke production.*

Ariel Square Four 4G Mk1 (1952)

Engine Air-cooled ohv eight-valve pushrod square-four

Capacity 997cc (65 x 75mm)

Maximum power 34bhp @ 5400rpm

Transmission Four-speed, chain final drive

Frame Steel twin downtube

Suspension Telescopic front; plunger rear

Brakes Drum front & rear

Weight 433lb (197kg)

Top speed 100mph (160km/h)

Indian Chief

The Chief led Indian's V-twin family for more than three decades, and remains an iconic machine due mainly to the unique style of later models. The 'Indian head' running light on a huge, skirted front mudguard reflected the character of the big, softly tuned, heavy and relatively low-tech Chief of the 1940s and early '50s; a bike that made up in style, comfort and cruising ability what it lacked in speed or handling prowess.

That late Chief's personality was very different to that of the original model, which was a much more performance-oriented machine. When Irish-born designer Charles B Franklin's initial Chief was launched in 1922, it used a frame based on that of the previous year's Scout model to hold a larger 998cc, side-valve V-twin engine developed from that of the long-running Powerplus. The Chief combined lively performance with good handling, but even so Indian promptly enlarged its engine to 1213cc (74ci) for the following year.

The so-called 'Big Chief' was a fine machine, its 40bhp output giving a top speed of 85mph (137km/h) in standard form. If featured leaf-spring front suspension, although a front brake was not added until 1928. By 1935 the Chief was available with the optional Y motor, which was more efficiently cooled due to its larger fins and aluminium instead of steel cylinder heads. The high-performance B or Bonneville powerplant, another option, incorporated hot cams, polished ports and precision timing, giving a top speed of 105mph (169km/h) that made the Chief one of the fastest bikes on the road.

Above: The late-model Chief's windscreen, running lights and crash-bars were all useful accessories but added to the big V-twin's already substantial weight.

Left: Huge skirted mudguards, tassels and an Indian's head light up front combined with the big V-twin engine to make the Chief instantly recognisable.

Indian struggled through the Depression of the 1930s, and lost ground to main rival Harley-Davidson, partly through its failure to introduce an overhead-valve replacement for the Chief's ageing side-valve powerplant. The Chief's emphasis on style was highlighted by the huge range of 24 standard paint schemes that were available, along with even more options at extra cost, after Indian had been taken over by the Du Pont chemical giant, which also produced paint.

The Chief was updated on numerous occasions, notably when being given the distinctive skirted mudguards in 1940, along with an uprated and cooler-running engine plus a new frame with plunger rear suspension. Girder forks had replaced the leaf-spring originals after World War II, and were in turn replaced by telescopics in 1950. At that time the engine was enlarged to 1311cc (80ci) by increasing its stroke to a huge 122mm, and Indian finally came into line with the rest of motorcycling by moving the hand-shift to the left side, and the throttle to the right.

The Chief of the early 1950s was stylish and comfortable, with those big mudguards, balloon tyres, a big 'buddy seat', and often an optional screen and leather panniers. But with a slow-revving 50bhp engine, standard three-speed box and over 550lb (250kg) of weight, it was not notably quick or agile. More importantly, sales were poor and Indian's financial problems had deepened following a failed attempt to sell small-capacity bikes. The last Chief left Indian's famous Springfield factory in 1953. Although the Indian name continued to be used on smaller bikes for some time, a big part of the US motorcycle scene had died.

Above: *Towards the end of its life the Chief was not particularly fast but it was stylish, comfortable and capable of effortless long-distance cruising.*

Indian Chief (1953)	
Engine	Air-cooled four-valve side-valve 42-degree V-twin
Capacity	1311cc (82.6 x 122mm)
Maximum power	50bhp @ 4800rpm
Transmission	Three-speed, chain final drive
Frame	Steel twin downtube
Suspension	Telescopic front; plunger rear
Brakes	Drum front & rear
Weight	570lb (259kg)
Top speed	90mph (145km/h)

BSA Gold Star DBD34 Clubman

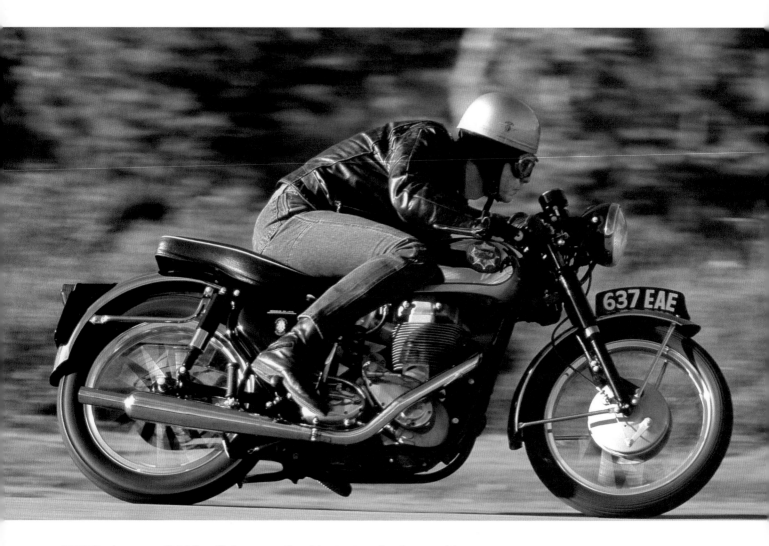

The lean, racy Gold Star Clubman was the ultimate street-legal competition bike of the 1950s. With its clip-on bars, chrome-panelled petrol tank, swept-back exhaust pipe and most of all its tuned 499cc single-cylinder powerplant, the 'Goldie' was fast, demanding and hugely popular – both with racers and with the road riders who valued its purposeful looks and thunderous 110mph (177km/h) performance.

Even the Gold Star's name was suitably evocative, for it referred to the lapel badge awarded to riders who lapped the banked Brooklands track at over 100mph (161km/h). The Gold Star model dated back to 1937, when BSA racer Wal Handley had earned the much-prized badge aboard the Birmingham firm's 500cc Empire Star.

The next year BSA released an uprated replica that it named the Gold Star in honour of Handley's lap. It featured a hotted-up engine incorporating an aluminium cylinder head and barrel, hand-polished inlet and exhaust ports,

Above: High-speed cornering was one of the Clubman Goldie's many strengths, thanks to its light weight, racy steering geometry and high quality suspension.

Above: The famous Gold Star tank badge was inspired by racer Wal Handley's 'ton-up' lap of Brooklands in 1937.

Above left: The classical Gold Star look included chrome-flanked fuel tank, big front drum brake, heavily finned single-pot motor, unfiltered carburettor and swept-back exhaust.

magnesium gearbox castings and other specially selected components. Peak power output was 28bhp, confirmed by the dyno chart that was issued with each machine. Despite having a relatively standard chassis for reasons of cost, the Gold Star handled very well and soon became popular.

One of the Goldie's greatest assets was its versatility. By 1950, BSA had introduced new versions of the single in 500cc ZB34 and 350cc ZB32 forms, both of which were competitive both on- and off-road. Their numerous factory options included four camshafts, four compression ratios (for use with different fuels from petrol to alcohol), and three alternative sets of gears: standard, road-racing or scrambling. Customers also had a choice of fuel tanks, exhaust systems and wheels.

In road-racing, in particular, the Gold Star built up a fearsome reputation. It dominated Clubman's (amateur) events at the Isle of Man TT, in both 500cc and 350cc classes. In the 1955 Junior TT, 33 of the 37 entrants were on Gold Stars, which led to the race being dropped from the programme after the following year.

The most famous Gold Star was the DBD34, which was launched in 1956, benefiting from BSA's development programme throughout the decade. Factory stars including Bill Nicholson had ridden Goldies to many wins in scrambles and trials, and introduced modifications including steeper steering geometry, swing-arm rear suspension (instead of plunger) and an improved front brake, which were incorporated into the production machine.

BSA's chief designer Bert Hopwood had also uprated the single-cylinder engine, notably two years earlier with the CB32 and CB34 models whose new top-ends had large finned cylinders. The DBD34 incorporated further improvements including a shorter, swept-back exhaust pipe, bigger Amal GP carburettor, and a close-ratio, four-speed gearbox that allowed a speed of almost 90mph (145km/h) in second.

In its classical, clip-on handlebarred Clubman form the Goldie was uncompromising and temperamental: often difficult to start, and too tall-geared and uncomfortable for slow-speed use. But the faster it went, the better it felt, and the uniquely single-minded BSA was much valued for its racetrack competitiveness and pure-bred roadgoing thrills alike. It remained in production until 1963.

BSA DBD34 Gold Star Clubman (1956)	
Engine	Air-cooled ohv two-valve pushrod single
Capacity	499cc (85 x 88mm)
Maximum power	42bhp @ 7000rpm
Transmission	Four-speed, chain final drive
Frame	Steel twin downtube
Suspension	Telescopic front; twin shocks rear
Brakes	Drum front & rear
Weight	384lb (174kg)
Top speed	110mph (177km/h)

Triumph T120 Bonneville

Triumph created its most famous and popular model in 1959 by fitting the existing 649cc Tiger 110 with a new cylinder head and twin carburettors. The resultant sports roadster was named T120 after its supposed top speed, and Bonneville after the salt flats in Utah, where a streamlined Triumph ridden by Johnny Allen had been timed at 214mph (344km/h) three years earlier. The fast and stylish 'Bonnie' would be the star of Triumph's range for years to come.

The original T120 required relatively little development. Its format of 649cc parallel twin, with pushrod valve operation, four-speed gearbox and 360-degree crankshaft, was identical to that of the Tiger 110. Even the tuning components were familiar, because in 1958 the Tiger had been available with an optional cylinder head incorporating splayed inlet ports, for fitment of twin carburettors, plus a list of performance parts including hot cams and Amal racing carbs.

Triumph's US distributors had requested a high-performance model, so the Meriden firm created the T120 by incorporating the sportier head plus a pair of Amal Monobloc carbs as standard fitment. The new twin's claimed peak output of 46bhp was 4bhp up on that of the Tiger. For its 1959 debut the Bonneville, which was put together hurriedly and was not featured in that year's Triumph catalogue, retained the Tiger's headlamp nacelle and touring handlebars.

As well as having thrilling acceleration to a 110mph (176km/h) top speed, the Bonneville was reasonably smooth. But the original T120's engine performance occasionally overwhelmed its single-downtube frame, making the bike prone to high-speed instability. For 1960 Triumph introduced a new twin-cradle frame with steeper steering geometry and shorter wheelbase, plus new forks and sportier styling featuring a separate headlamp shell and smaller mudguards.

Above and below left: The T120 Bonnie's lean lines and rev-happy engine combined to make it one of the most popular bikes on the road throughout the '60s.

Following some frame-cracking problems the chassis was strengthened for 1961. Triumph updated the Bonnie regularly over the next decade and created several variations. The basic home-market T120 was joined by the T120C competition model and a stylish if less practical export version, featuring high handlebars and a small fuel tank. In 1963, the factory introduced a redesigned 'unit' 650 with engine and gearbox combined instead of the previous separate or pre-unit layout.

The Bonneville's handling was never as highly rated as that of its Norton rivals, but the Triumph's all-round performance was hard to beat. That was also true on a racetrack, including the Isle of Man. John Hartle won the production TT in 1967, and Malcolm Uphill repeated the feat two years later, setting the first production 100mph (160km/h) lap in the process. The T120 also took four wins in the prestigious 500-mile (805km) production races at Thruxton and Brands Hatch, with riders including Triumph's tester Percy Tait.

In 1971 the Bonnie was redesigned with a taller, so-called 'oil-in-frame' chassis, which was heavily criticised until hastily revised to lower the seat height. By 1972, Triumph had produced an estimated 250,000 Bonnevilles. The T120's reign ended the following year, when engine capacity was increased to 744cc, producing the torquier but less smooth-running T140 Bonneville.

Triumph T120 Bonneville (1961)	
Engine	Air-cooled four-valve ohv pushrod parallel twin
Capacity	649cc (71 x 82mm)
Maximum power	46bhp @ 6500rpm
Transmission	Four-speed, chain final drive
Frame	Steel twin downtube
Suspension	Telescopic front; twin shocks rear
Brakes	Drum front & rear
Weight	402lb (183kg) wet
Top speed	110mph (177km/h)

Below: The Bonneville's visual appeal matched its performance – which is boosted in this 1962-model's case by flat bars and filterless Amal carbs.

Harley-Davidson Sportster

O n its introduction in 1957, Harley-Davidson's Sportster justified its name with performance that made it one of the fastest and hardest-accelerating bikes on the road. The original Sportster was notable for its overhead valve operation, replacing the side-valve layout of Harley's existing 883cc K-series V-twin. Other features included short-stroke engine dimensions and bigger valves, which helped give a 40bhp peak output and a top speed of over 100mph (161km/h).

The Harley was a stylish machine, too, with two-tone paintwork, chrome-covered rear shocks, and the 'Sportster' name cast into its engine's primary drive cover. Frame and cycle parts came from its K-series predecessor, and gave respectably good handling and braking. It was as well built as it was fast, and quickly became popular, selling almost twice as many units in 1957 as the Model K had the previous year. As an alternative to its standard form, it could be adapted with accessories including windscreen, crash bars, luggage rack and panniers.

Harley introduced numerous Sportster variants in subsequent years, some incorporating a diminutive peanut fuel tank originally fitted to the firm's 125cc Hummer two-stroke. There was the off-road XLC, stripped of lights and with open pipes; and the XLH with its hotted-up engine. Fastest of all was the XLCH: originally a California-only dirtbike with tuned motor and no lights, before in 1959 being adapted to create a street-legal machine. Its style, performance and engaging V-twin character highlighted the raw appeal that would make the Sportster a long-lived legend.

Above: The Sportster's 883cc overhead-valve V-twin engine gave straight-line performance that few 1957 rivals could match.

Below: Chrome-covered rear shocks, two-tone paintwork and the Sportster name cast into its engine cover all added to the Harley's undeniable visual appeal.

Matchless G12

The Matchless G12, like its twin the AJS Model 31, was one of the more successful products of the badge engineering that saw near-identical machines marketed with different names following the merger that resulted in the formation of Associated Motor Cycles (AMC). Matchless, the old firm whose co-founder Charlie Collier had won the single-cylinder race at the first ever Isle of Man TT in 1907, had taken over AJS of Wolverhampton in 1931. Production continued at the Matchless factory in south London, and both marques' names continued to be used.

When the 646cc G12/Model 31 was introduced in 1959, it traced its lineage back ten years to the Matchless G9, a 498cc parallel twin also sold as the AJS Model 20. That was a flexible and sweet-running bike whose engine was bored out to 592cc in 1956, creating the G11/Model 30. The engine could not be bored out any further, so for the G12/Model 31 AMC developed a longer-stroke crankshaft that took capacity to 646cc.

The G12's additional capacity gave even more mid-range punch. The bike made a fairly popular all-rounder, thanks to its lively acceleration, impressive low-rev docility, and respectable top speed of just over 100mph (161km/h). It also handled well and was reliable, both in standard form or as the slightly more expensive De Luxe, which incorporated an uprated ignition and quickly-detachable rear wheel. Unfortunately the same could not be said of the hotted-up G12 CSR, which stormed to a top speed of 108mph (174km/h) but vibrated and frequently broke.

Above: Matchless fitted a new long-stroke crankshaft to give the G12's parallel-twin powerplant a capacity of 646cc.

Left: This 1959-model G12 De Luxe features the slim rear shocks that replaced the distinctively fat 'jampot' design in 1957, but not the twin-downtube frame that was introduced in 1960.

Matchless G12 De Luxe (1959)	
Engine	Air-cooled ohv pushrod four-valve parallel twin
Capacity	646cc (72 x 79.3mm)
Maximum power	35bhp @ 6000rpm
Transmission	Four-speed, chain final drive
Frame	Steel single downtube
Suspension	Telescopic front; twin shocks rear
Brakes	Drum front & rear
Weight	400lb (182kg)
Top speed	102mph (164km/h)

Honda C71

Honda's well-built and reliable small-capacity models, led by the C71, heralded a new motorcycling era when they reached Europe and the United States in the late 1950s. The C71 and its Japanese-market-only predecessor the C70 were inspired by German firm NSU's rapid Rennmax twin-cylinder racers, which had impressed Soichiro Honda on his visit to Europe a few years earlier. Honda's 247cc engine used a single overhead camshaft, unlike the dohc NSUs. It produced 18bhp and featured an electric starter.

The name on the partly-chromed tank was Dream, which Honda had used ever since his firm's first wholly built machine, the 98cc Model D of 1949. The frame, front forks and swing-arm were made from pressed-steel sections, which had the advantage of being quick and inexpensive to produce. The forks were short, leading-link units with spring and damper units inside the pressings. The rear shock units were rectangular in section and, along with the huge mudguards, contributed to the bike's old-fashioned appearance.

Although the C71 was no sports bike it had very acceptable performance, with a top speed of 80mph (129km/h). The soft and simple suspension gave mediocre handling but the Honda's brakes were impressive. So were features including its indicators, comprehensive tool kit, reliability and ease of maintenance. The twin was a high-quality package, albeit an expensive one by 250cc standards. Few were sold in the West, but with the C71 and its contemporaries Honda laid the foundations for Japan's future motorcycling dominance.

Honda C71 (1960)	
Engine	Air-cooled sohc four-valve parallel twin
Capacity	247cc (54 x 54mm)
Maximum power	18bhp @ 7400rpm
Transmission	Four-speed, chain final drive
Frame	Pressed-steel spine
Suspension	Leading-link front; twin shocks rear
Brakes	Drum front & rear
Weight	354lb (161kg)
Top speed	80mph (129km/h)

Above: The C71 was solidly engineered and performed quite well but its old-fashioned look did not increase Honda's chance of success in export markets.

Left: Like its frame and swing-arm, the Honda's leading-axle front forks were made from pressed steel, which was cheap to produce but provided neither style not optimum performance.

Honda CB72

The fast and sporty CB72 did more than any other bike to improve the image of Japanese machines in the early 1960s. This 247cc four-stroke parallel twin was the model that proved Honda was getting serious. Until the CB72 reached export markets in 1962, Honda's roadsters had typically been well made but curiously styled and heavy. The new twin – known as the Dream Super Sport in Britain and the Hawk in the US – was very different.

The CB72 was the sporty version of Honda's three-model 250cc range. It had low handlebars, a thinly padded dual seat, and an innovative instrument panel incorporating speedometer and rev-counter whose needles rotated in opposite directions. Twin carbs helped give a peak output of 24bhp. The chassis changes were even more important. In place of a pressed-steel frame was a new and more rigid tubular construction, based on that of Honda's works racers. Traditional leading-link front suspension was replaced by telescopics, with a pair of round-section shocks at the rear.

Those features gave the CB72 a much more racy and modern look, and riding it did not disappoint. Top speed was a genuine 90mph (145km/h), with acceleration to match. The Honda was stable at speed, and handled well thanks to reasonably firm suspension. Its brakes, twin leading-shoe drums at each end, were powerful too. The CB72 impressed not only with its speed and chassis performance but also with its quality and reliability. It proved once and for all that Honda could made quick, fine-handling and stylish bikes.

Above: The Honda's sweet-revving and reliable 247cc parallel-twin engine used a single overhead camshaft to produce a maximum of 24bhp.

Below: The CB72's tubular-steel frame, telescopic forks and conventional rear shocks contrasted with the old-fashioned chassis design of previous Honda roadsters.

Yamaha YDS-2

Above: The little Yamaha's agile handling was almost as vital to its appeal as its lively straight-line performance.

The YDS-2 made a big contribution towards establishing not just Yamaha but small-capacity Japanese two-strokes in general as a popular form of transport. The little 250cc twin was rev-happy, loud, reasonably cheap and impressively reliable. Most of all, it was fast enough to outrun every 250cc rival following its arrival in export markets in 1962.

Parent company Nippon Gakki, best known for musical instruments, had turned to motorcycle production only in 1955 as a way of utilising machinery that had been used to make propellers in World War II. Yamaha's first models, such as the 125cc YA-1 or 'Red Dragonfly' single, and the 250cc YD-2, the firm's first twin, had confirmed the firm's expertise at building small-capacity two-strokes. But those bikes and sportier 250cc YDS-1 had been sold mainly on the home market.

The YDS-2 changed all that. It was this lively little twin that began the Japanese firm's long run of success with small- and medium-capacity two-strokes. Its straight-line speed came from a simple air-cooled, piston-ported two-stroke parallel twin engine. Capacity was 246cc; claimed peak output was 25bhp at 7500rpm. A pair of Amal carburettors provided the fuel – a mixture of petrol and oil that, in old-fashioned style, had to be pre-mixed in the tank at every fill up.

Chassis layout was typical of the 1960s, with a steel twin-cradle frame, simple front forks, twin rear shocks and 18-inch wire-spoked wheels. The styling was

Below: The YDS-2's styling owed much to Yamahas of the late 1950s. The tuning fork tank badge was a reference to the firm's production of musical instruments.

neat and restrained, Yamaha's tuning-fork badges sharing space on the tank with rubber kneepads.

There was no doubting the YDS-2's ability to produce thrilling acceleration and the 90mph (145km/h) top speed claimed in contemporary adverts. The 180-degree-crankshaft motor was smooth, too, just about justifying the 'twin cylinder – smooth as a four' comment that came under the advertising headline 'Greatest Yamaha Ever Built'. Chassis performance was nowhere near as impressive as the engine, but the YDS-2's weight of just 312lb (142kg) helped make it agile, and its brakes were highly rated. Even its stability and general handling were praised in contemporary reports, despite soft and wallowy suspension that was described by US magazine Cycle World as 'too soft for anything but touring'.

Like the other Japanese manufacturers, Yamaha would take more than another ten years to get its machines' handling really sorted out. But it's a reflection of the firm's determination to improve its product that just a year later the YDS-2 was replaced by the YDS-3 – featuring not only an automatic Autolube engine lubrication system and a couple of extra horsepower, but also stiffer suspension at both front and rear.

Larger-capacity models followed, too, starting with the 305cc YM-1 of 1965 and the 350cc YR-1 of two years later. On the racetrack Yamaha's Phil Read won four 250cc titles, and other riders including Finnish ace Jarno Saarinen continued the firm's Grand Prix domination. In just a few years, Yamaha had risen from comparative obscurity to become one of the world's leading manufacturers. The YDS-2 had played an important part in that success.

Yamaha YDS-2 (1962)	
Engine	Air-cooled two-stroke parallel twin
Capacity	246cc (56 x 50mm)
Maximum power	25bhp @ 7500rpm
Transmission	Four-speed, chain final drive
Frame	Steel cradle
Suspension	Telescopic front, twin shocks rear
Weight	312lb (142kg)
Top speed	90mph (145km/h)

Below: The Yamaha's forks and shocks were criticised for being too soft in contemporary tests, but the Yamaha's twin leading-shoe front drum brake was praised.

BSA Rocket Gold Star

BSA's A10 line of 'pre-unit' 646cc parallel twins ended in spectacular style with the Rocket Gold Star, which housed the powerful twin-pot motor from the Super Rocket in a high-quality chassis derived from that of the single-cylinder Gold Star. The factory RGS, launched in 1962, was inspired by a one-off special that Oxfordshire BSA dealer Eddie Dow had built for a customer. A few modifications were made for production, but the blend of top-class engine and chassis performance was very much intact.

The uprated engine incorporated an aluminium cylinder head with increased 9:1 compression ration, hotter camshaft, and racing-style magneto with manual advance-retard adjustment. Peak output was raised slightly to 46bhp, or 50bhp when fitted with the optional Gold Star style racing silencer. The chassis was of equally high specification, including Gold Star gaitered forks, large-capacity alloy fuel tank, close-ratio gearbox, siamesed exhaust system, humped racing seat, alloy wheel rims, and a big front drum brake.

The result was a stunningly purposeful machine that was one of the ultimate café racers. It roared to a genuine top speed of 115mph (145km/h), and was ideally suited to high-speed runs when in home-market specification with Gold Star style clip-on bars, instead of the higher bars fitted to export models. Handling and braking were also very highly rated. At the end of 1963, BSA halted production to concentrate on its new 654cc line of unit-construction twins. The Rocket Goldie had been a fine way for the A10 line to end.

Above: *The rev-counter, on right, was an optional extra that was popular with many Rocket Gold Star riders, as were rearset footrests and alloy wheel rims.*

Below: *This 1963-model Rocket Goldie is an American-market machine, with higher bars and a smaller tank than the bikes built for the British café-racer crowd.*

BMW R69S

For refinement, effortless high-speed cruising ability and quality of construction, few bikes of the 1960s came close to matching BMW's R69S. But the 594cc boxer earned its reputation only after overcoming a shaky start, because, following its introduction in 1960, it suffered a series of engine failures that came as an unpleasant surprise to BMW, which had a long history of robust and reliable horizontally opposed twins.

The German marque's pushrod-operated boxer engine layout traced its ancestry to 1936, and the 494cc R5 model with which BMW had introduced overhead valves to its range, alongside the previous side-valve twins. Initially the R69S gave no sign of trouble, as it scored a series of track successes. In 1961, an S-model modified with taller gearing averaged 109mph (175km/h) to break the world 12-hour and 24-hour records. In the same year, the R69S was ridden to victory in both the Barcelona 24-hour race and the Thruxton 500-mile (805km) event for production machines.

The R69S was a sports machine, designed for hard and fast riding, and its 42bhp engine's problems were triggered by sustained high-speed riding, especially on German autobahns. Once the trouble was cured, with stronger crankcases and a vibration damper on the crankshaft, the boxer cruised with a pleasantly smooth feel at 80mph (129km/h), with performance in hand to a top speed of 110mph (177km/h). It was also stable and comfortable, although heavier than rival British twins. It remained in production until 1969, when over 11,000 had been built.

Above: By the time this R69S was built in 1964, BMW had modified its 594cc boxer engine with a crankshaft-mounted vibration damper that dramatically improved its reliability.

Below: The BMW's thick dual seat helped to make it comfortable, and the bike also handled well thanks partly to its firm and well-damped Earles forks.

Dresda Triton

The Triton was the supreme hybrid of 1960s British motorcycling: a blend of Triumph parallel-twin powerplant and Norton Featherbed-framed chassis that provided the speed and handling ability to outrun just about anything else on the road. Many firms and individuals assembled Tritons over the years, using a variety of motors and frames. Of them all, the best known were the machines that were built and successfully raced, both in Britain and abroad, by London dealer Dresda Autos.

Precise origins of the first Triton are unclear, because several similar machines were constructed independently in the 1950s. One was built by London-based racer/engineer Doug Clark, who fitted a Triumph 650cc engine into a Manx Norton frame in 1954. The bike was used both on road and track, as Clark rode it to the circuits where he was competing. Triumph was reportedly unhappy. The firm wrote to Clark threatening legal action if he continued with the project, and told its London dealers to refuse to sell him engine spares.

It was easy to understand the Triton's appeal in the early 1960s, when Norton and Triumph twins were among the fastest machines on the road. Triumph's 650cc Tiger 110 had held a straight-line advantage over its 600cc rival the Norton Dominator 99, and by the time Norton's more powerful 650SS arrived in 1962, Triumph's reputation for speed was secure. But Norton's Featherbed frame and Roadholder forks were superior to their Triumph equivalents, and also came with an impressive racing pedigree.

By providing the best of both worlds, the Triton became the ultimate high-performance parallel twin. Machines varied considerably, featuring different fuel tanks, instruments, seats, suspension parts, and exhaust systems. As well as Triumph's twin-carburettor 650cc Bonneville engine, Triton builders used 500cc

Above: Key to the Triton is its combination of Triumph parallel-twin engine and Norton Featherbed frame. The large-radius rear curve shows this Featherbed is from a Manx single.

Left: This Triton's classical café-racer look is enhanced by clip-on bars, exposed fork springs, big twin leading-shoe front drum brake, humped seat and unfiltered Amal carbs.

motors, and later the 750cc unit too. Norton's Featherbed frame came in original Wideline or later Slimline form, as well as being sourced from the Manx single.

One thing that almost all Tritons shared was the classical look, comprising long alloy fuel tank, clip-on handlebars, rearset footrests, and most of all the compact parallel-twin Triumph motor surrounded by the Featherbed frame's distinctively curved steel tubes. If the secret of the Triton's success was that it combined the best British engine and chassis, it's also true that much of its appeal came from its lean and uncluttered style.

The Triton's popularity leapt when firms including Dresda began producing conversion kits and complete machines. Dresda boss Dave Degens was a leading racer, and his victory (with co-rider Rex Butcher) on a Triton in the 24-hour race at Montjuic Park in Barcelona in 1965 boosted demand. Degens, who won at Barcelona again on a similar machine five years later, estimates that his firm built over 500 Tritons in the 1960s and early '70s, plus many Featherbed-style frames around which owners assembled Tritons of their own.

Even the Triton could not compete against more powerful Japanese and Italian machines in the 1970s. But its reputation as motorcycling's finest hybrid, and one of the great high-performance machines, is very much intact.

Dresda Triton (1965)	
Engine	Air-cooled ohv four-valve Triumph parallel twin
Capacity	649cc (71 x 82mm)
Maximum power	50bhp @ 6500rpm
Transmission	Four-speed, chain final drive
Frame	Steel twin cradle Norton Featherbed
Suspension	Telescopic front; twin shocks rear
Brakes	Drum front & rear
Weight	350lb (159kg)
Top speed	120mph (192km/h)

Opposite: This 1965-model Triton, powered by a 650cc Bonneville engine, was one of many hundred built by London dealer Dresda, which continued production into the 21st century.

Velocette Venom Thruxton

The fastest and most glamorous of Velocette's long line of 500cc singles was the Venom Thruxton. Introduced in 1965, it was essentially a tuned and race-kitted version of the Venom, Velocette's standard large-capacity model. Since the start of the decade, the Venom had been available in race-ready 'Clubman' spec, featuring clip-on bars and high-compression engine. In 1964 the Birmingham firm had also introduced a high-performance kit incorporating a new cylinder head plus large Amal Grand Prix carburettor.

A year later Velocette fitted the Venom Clubman with the performance kit to create the Thruxton, which also featured a big silver-painted petrol tank with a cut-out for the carb. Other features included a humped racing seat, rearset footrests, alloy wheel rims, and twin leading-shoe front drum brake with a scoop for cooling air. The Thruxton was expensive but it had the performance to match. The 41bhp engine gave a top speed of 105mph (169km/h), plus flexibility and 90mph (145km/h) cruising ability.

The Thruxton was not every rider's idea of a fast motorcycle. The single was often difficult to start, and was prone to loose bolts due to vibration. Its generally sound handling was compromised by occasional instability when ridden hard. But many Velocette enthusiasts were delighted by its unique blend of uncompromising character and race-derived performance, and the Thruxton sold well. Sadly for Velocette, even this ultimate single could not save the marque following its disastrous decision to produce scooters and the two-stroke LE commuter bike. Production finally ended in 1971.

Above: The Thruxton, with its racy lines and powerful 500cc engine, continued a line of sporty Velocette singles that stretched back to TT-winning machines of the 1920s.

Below: This Thruxton's notable features include its big twin leading-shoe drum, trademark Velo fishtail silencer, and the tank cut-out for the big Amal carburettor.

Bridgestone 350 GTR

Until the late 1960s Japanese industrial giant Bridgestone backed up its tyre manufacture by building a string of high-quality two-stroke motorcycles. The best of them was the 350 GTR, whose sophisticated 345cc parallel-twin engine differed from rival two-strokes by featuring rotary disc valve induction, which gave more precise control than the simpler piston ports normally used. This helped the GTR to an impressive peak power output of 37bhp, which it complemented with sound handling and high production quality.

The stylish and lightweight GTR was particularly notable for its acceleration, and could keep up with almost any other bike from a standing start. The Bridgestone was also stable at speed, with a notably refined feel. Its six-speed gearbox's tall top ratio kept maximum speed down to about 95mph (153km/h). But the motor's broad spread of torque, combined with the rubber-mounted powerplant's smoothness, meant that roadgoing speed was limited more frequently by the exposed riding position than by engine performance.

The GTR also handled very well, with the help of a rigid twin-cradle steel frame, plus firm and efficient suspension that typified Bridgestone's generally high-quality construction. Braking was impressive, too, due mainly to the reliable power of the twin leading-shoe front drum. If the GTR had a weakness it was price, because the refined twin was significantly more expensive than its Japanese two-stroke rivals. Relatively few were sold before Bridgestone abandoned motorcycle production in 1969 to concentrate on manufacturing the tyres for which the company is still well known.

Above: *Raised handlebars and a tall top gear didn't help the GTR's high-speed performance, but the twin was still good for a respectable 95mph (153km/h).*

Left: *This immaculate GTR highlights the neat design and high build quality for which Bridgestone was known before the firm halted motorcycle production in 1969.*

Bridgestone 350 GTR (1966)	
Engine	Air-cooled two-stroke parallel twin
Capacity	345cc (61 x 59mm)
Maximum power	37bhp @ 7500rpm
Transmission	Six-speed, chain final drive
Frame	Steel twin cradle
Suspension	Telescopic front; twin shocks rear
Brakes	Drum front & rear
Weight	330lb (150kg)
Top speed	95mph (153km/h)

Norton Commando

Norton's Commando was one of the most famous and best loved of British bikes, its success stemming from the way that its innovative chassis used rubber mountings to reduce the vibration generated by its parallel-twin engine. That allowed the Commando's rider to make the most of the bike's engaging blend of torquey engine and capable handling, to which it added good looks and a generally high level of reliability.

The first Commando, launched in 1968, was a striking machine whose streamlined tailpiece earned the designation 'Fastback'. Its 745cc pushrod-operated power-plant was based on that of Norton's previous Atlas, with cylinders angled slightly forward instead of vertical. Other modifications including increased compression ratio boosted claimed maximum output to 58bhp, and the motor also featured a new single-plate diaphragm clutch.

The Commando's big advance was its new chassis, whose Isolastic system of rubber mounting was designed to tackle the vibration that had plagued larger-capacity parallel twins including the Atlas. The system was developed by a team headed by former Rolls-Royce engineer Dr Stefan Bauer. The frame comprised a large main spine plus twin downtubes. Rubber-mounted rear engine plates, isolated the motor while allowing the frame's spine to counter torsional stresses.

Provided its rubber bushes were well maintained, the Isolastic frame lived up to its name by significantly reducing vibration. It helped maintain Norton's traditionally high standard of handling, backed up by efficient Roadholder forks and Girling shocks. And the Commando also had the engine performance to match, with storming acceleration to a top speed of 115mph (184km/h). It was rapturously received, winning the prestigious Motor Cycle News Machine of the Year competition five years in a row.

The Commando was also a hit in the US, where it was sold with high, wide handlebars. Norton developed special versions for the US market, notably the 1971-model Commando SS, a street scrambler with a small fuel tank and high-level pipes, and the Hi-Rider with its chopper-style seat and high bars. For sportier riders there was the Combat Commando, which had flatter bars to complement its hotted-up 65bhp motor. But the Combat was an unreliable disaster because its engine could not handle the extra power.

Commandos were raced successfully in the early 1970s, despite generally being down on power compared to most rivals. Norton's works racer/engineer Peter Williams developed the Commando Formula 750, whose steel monocoque frame gave advantages in both weight and aerodynamics, and rode the innovative twin to victory against Japanese opposition in the 1973 Formula 750 TT.

Norton also continued to develop the roadgoing model, notably in 1973, when its engine was bored-out to create the Commando 850. This was produced in standard Roadster and larger-tanked Interstate options. The bigger motor's added torque gave a useful performance boost but the ageing parallel twin's limitations were highlighted by Norton's struggle to add a reliable electric starter. By the mid-1970s parent company Norton Villiers Triumph had slipped into financial problems. Production of the by then outdated Commando continued until 1977.

Above: This immaculate Commando features the long tailpiece that earned the first model the name 'Fastback', and has a disc front brake rather than the original drum.

Opposite: The rubber-mounted Commando engine's smoothness encouraged its rider to make the most of its performance — by keeping the needles of both speedometer and rev-counter spinning.

Norton Commando (1968)

Engine Air-cooled ohv four-valve pushrod
parallel-twin

Capacity 745cc (73 x 89mm)

Maximum power 58bhp @ 6800rpm

Transmission Four-speed, chain final drive

Frame Steel spine with twin downtubes

Suspension Telescopic front; twin shock rear

Brakes Drum front and rear

Weight 420lb (190kg)

Top speed 115mph (184km/h)

Harley-Davidson FX Super Glide

The Super Glide was a vital part of Harley-Davidson's survival through difficult times in the early 1970s. Harley design director Willie G Davidson's striking V-twin, also known as the FX1200, is also regarded by many enthusiasts as the forerunner of the 'factory custom' – manufacturers' versions of the choppers and cruisers that were then being assembled by countless individuals. The Glide's format of large-capacity cruiser with a relatively sporty style pointed the Milwaukee firm in a new and important direction.

Essentially the Super Glide was a combination of the V-twin engine and rear end of Harley's giant Electra Glide and the front end of the (relatively) lightweight Sportster. Its powerplant was the 1200cc (74 cubic inch) Shovelhead unit, as fitted to the big tourer, with a Sportster-style two-into-one exhaust system. The electric starter was omitted, allowing fitment of a smaller battery on the right side. Styling included a broad fuel tank and the option of paintwork in patriotic red, white and blue, but was most notable for the 'boat-tail', a large glass-fibre seat/tail section.

The boat-tail proved unpopular and was promptly dropped for the 1972 sales season, but the Super Glide itself was a success. In subsequent years it became more performance oriented, being uprated with features including a slimmer tank, firmer suspension, disc brakes and an electric starter. The changes made the Glide more popular with each year, and it also formed the inspiration for other models, notably the Low Rider of 1977, that played a key part in Harley's revival.

Harley-Davidson FX Super Glide (1971)	
Engine	Air-cooled ohv pushrod four-valve 45-degree V-twin
Capacity	1208cc (87 x 101mm)
Maximum power	65bhp @ 5500rpm
Transmission	Four-speed, chain final drive
Frame	Tubular steel
Suspension	Telescopic front; twin shocks rear
Brakes	Drum front & rear
Weight	560lb (254kg)
Top speed	110mph (177km/h)

Below: The Super Glide's patriotic red, white and blue paint scheme was well received but many dealers removed the 'boat-tail' rear section, which wasn't. In 1972 Harley replaced it with a standard rear mudguard, triggering the Glide's rise in popularity.

BMW R75/5

The revised, so-called 'toaster tank' R75/5 that BMW launched in 1972, with its small, white-painted, chrome-sided petrol tank, was early evidence of the German firm's determination to appeal to more sporting riders than those who had previously been attracted by its conservative range of lookalike boxers with their big black tanks. On its launch three years earlier, the new-generation R75/5 had already broken the mould, being available in a choice of paint schemes, and abandoning the Earles fork front suspension system used in previous years.

Engine layout remained BMW's traditional air-cooled, two-valves-per-cylinder, pushrod-operated flat twin. But the 745cc unit's redesigned top section incorporated an electric starter and air filter housing, and other changes included alloy barrels and a strengthened shaft-drive transmission. The new frame had a single large-diameter top tube and twin downtubes, which curved upwards behind the engine, giving a look similar to that of Norton's Featherbed.

The R75/5 produced 50bhp and was respectably light at 418lb (190kg), which helped make it quick off the mark despite having only four gears. It cruised smoothly at 80mph (129km/h) and had a maximum speed of 110mph (176km/h). Front and rear drum brakes gave powerful stopping, and in bends the R75/5 lived up to the German marque's reputation for stable if less than sporty handling. More than its cornering speed, though, it was the BMW's blend of performance, practicality, build quality and long-distance comfort that endeared it to the minority of motorcyclists fortunate enough to be able to afford one.

Above: The chrome-sided 'toaster tank' gave the R75/5 a distinctive look, but proved unpopular with BMW customers and was soon dropped.

Below: Bing CV carbs helped the redesigned 745cc boxer motor produce 50bhp.

Honda CB750

The CB750's unprecedented combination of performance, sophistication and reliability made it a huge hit and launched the 1970s superbike era. Honda's powerful and smooth-running four had a massive influence on the bikes that followed. Such was its impact that it is widely accepted as the most important motorcycle ever built.

Sheer performance was a key aspect of the Honda's appeal. Vivid acceleration to a top speed of over 120mph (193km/h) put the four far ahead of most rivals on its launch in 1969. But more than pure speed, it was the Honda's level of refinement that made it special: its electric starter, disc front brake, five-speed gearbox, and most of all the four-cylinder powerplant and its eye-catching quartet of chromed exhaust pipes.

The 736cc, air-cooled engine's design was influenced by Honda's magical World Championship winning multi-cylinder racebikes of the 1960s, although the roadster's layout of single overhead camshaft and total of eight valves did not match the

Above: The CB750's unprecedented blend of overhead-cam four-cylinder powerplant and disc front brake caused a sensation when the bike was released. Honda's designers emphasised the engine layout by adding an attractive and free-breathing four-pipe exhaust system.

Left: Performance was stunning by early-'70s standards, and unlike most bikes the Honda was happy at high speed for as long as its rider could hold on.

Below: This CB750 was the first registered in Britain, in January 1970. The model was called the CB750 K0 in the US, where it was released in mid-1969.

exotic racers with their twin cams and four valves per cylinder. Peak output was an impressive 67bhp at 8000rpm, with strong low-rev performance plus a smoothness that most rival machines could not approach.

Equally importantly, the four-cylinder unit was notably robust and well engineered. By the time of the CB750's arrival, a generation of motorcyclists had grown up on smaller Hondas, and were confident that the Japanese firm's bikes would be reliable, and would have good electrics and no oil leaks. The CB750 exceeded expectations on all counts.

Chassis layout was based on a steel, twin-cradle frame that held the engine with cylinders angled slightly forward. The initial four was designed mainly as an all-rounder for the US market, and was a physically large bike with high bars and a wide seat. But, despite the exposed and upright riding position, it was well suited to cruising at speed.

When it was ridden hard, the Honda's combination of power, weight and flex-prone steel frame resulted in some instability. But most of the time it handled well enough, helped by firm suspension. Its powerful and fade-free single disc front brake gave an advantage in both image and performance over rival machines' drum brakes.

The Honda's competitive price also helped it to become an instant commercial success, especially in the US where most of the early production was sold. Honda even got a boost in 1970 when veteran racer Dick Mann won the Daytona 200 on a modified CB750. Sales took off in Europe, too, when the four arrived in early 1970. Rivals including Triumph's Trident and BSA's Rocket 3 triples seemed not merely outdated but the products of a previous generation.

Honda acted relatively slowly to update the original four, which was detuned slightly in subsequent years due to emissions regulations, and lost its performance lead when Kawasaki's 903cc, dohc Z1 arrived in 1973. But a variety of CB750 models remained popular, as did smaller variants including the CB500. The original four will long be remembered for transforming motorcycling and starting the superbike generation.

Honda CB750 (1969)

Engine	Air-cooled sohc eight-valve four
Capacity	736cc (61 x 63mm)
Maximum power	67bhp @ 8000rpm
Transmission	Five-speed, chain final drive
Frame	Steel twin downtube
Suspension	Telescopic front; twin shocks rear
Brakes	Single disc front; drum rear
Weight	506lb (230kg) wet
Top speed	123mph (198km/h)

Triumph X-75 Hurricane

With its trio of exhaust pipes plus a uniquely curvaceous tank-seat unit that highlighted its 740cc three-cylinder motor, Triumph's X-75 Hurricane was one of the most stylish bikes of the early 1970s – and one of the hardest accelerating. The Hurricane concept originated with Triumph's importer in the US, where the T150 Trident's angular styling was unpopular. The new triple was shaped in the States, without Triumph's knowledge, by young freelance designer Craig Vetter, later famous for making fairings and luggage.

Vetter replaced the original bodywork with a slender fibreglass form that blended the fuel tank into the sidepanel area. The tiny gas tank was impractical, but the visual effect was stunning. The 60bhp engine's cylinder head fins were enlarged to add visual impact, and gearing was lowered. Handlebars were raised, front forks were lengthened, and many other parts were modified. Exhaust downpipes slanted across the front of the motor, then ran back to the bank of upswept silencers on the right.

Acceleration in the lower gears was terrific, thanks to the Hurricane's relatively light weight and short gearing. Its 115mph (185km/h) top speed was 10mph (16km/h) down on that of the Trident, but standing quarter-mile time was half a second quicker. High-speed handling was dubious due to the bike's combination of high bars and kicked-out forks. But the X-75 was less about performance than style and attitude. The Trident was a better all-round bike but the Hurricane's looks and acceleration earned it a cult following, especially in the US.

Above: The Hurricane's unique exhaust system emphasised the bike's three-cylinder engine layout.

Below: Vetter's flowing tank-seat unit gave the triple an unmistakable look, enhanced by lengthened forks and the trio of exhaust pipes.

MV Agusta 750 Sport

MV Agusta's multi-cylinder racebikes dominated the 500cc World Championship during the 1960s, but it was only with the arrival of the 750 Sport in 1973 that the Italian marque brought that glamour and performance to the street. MV boss Count Domenico Agusta had been reluctant to dilute his team's achievements with a roadgoing four, and had eventually released a 600cc tourer with curious styling, shaft final drive and modest performance. It had been an expensive failure.

The 750 Sport was totally different – an aggressive superbike with bright paintwork, clip-on bars and a humped racing seat. Its 743cc engine was based on that of the tourer, with gear drive to twin overhead cams. Unfiltered Dell'Orto carburettors, high-compression pistons and a quartet of shiny megaphone pipes helped lift peak output to 65bhp. Even the Sport had shaft final drive, and a frame that derived from the tourer rather than MV's racers. But it benefited from exotic cycle parts including Ceriani suspension, alloy wheel rims and Grimeca brakes; initially a big drum and later twin discs.

Straight-line performance didn't match factory claims, the true top speed being a rather disappointing 115mph (185km/h). Handling was also compromised by the bike's shaft drive and 506lb (230kg) of weight. But the Sport delivered strong and smooth acceleration, with a glorious howl from its exhaust, plus handling and braking performance that exceeded those of most superbikes. The hand-built MV was hugely expensive, but for the small number of riders who could afford one it was an utterly exhilarating machine.

Above: Fitting MV's optional full fairing hid the gorgeous dohc four-cylinder engine but enhanced the Sport's authentic race-replica look.

Above: The Sport was magnificently fast and loud but didn't match MV's performance claims.

Kawasaki Z1

Kawasaki's Z1 four took superbike performance to a different level when it howled onto the scene in 1973. Its 903cc engine was not only considerably larger than the 736cc unit of the Honda CB750 that had revolutionised motorcycling four years earlier, it also boasted twin overhead camshafts that helped give a maximum output of 82bhp – fully 15bhp up on the sohc Honda's figure. The result was a stunningly rapid bike that was in a class of its own for speed and adrenaline production.

Ironically it was the CB750 that led directly to the Z1's engine capacity and resultant power output, because in 1968 Kawasaki's engineers had been well on the way to completing a 750cc four project – nicknamed New York Steak – before being shocked by the CB750's unveiling. The Honda's subsequent success gave Kawasaki all the incentive needed to create a significantly more powerful and faster machine.

Below: As if the Z1's fearsome performance was not enough of an attraction, the Kawasaki was also very stylish, highlighted by its muscular dohc engine and the neat duck-tail rear end.

Kawasaki Z1 (1973)	
Engine Air-cooled dohc eight-valve four	
Capacity 903cc (66 x 66mm)	
Maximum power 82bhp @ 8500rpm	
Transmission Five-speed, chain final drive	
Frame Steel twin downtube	
Suspension Telescopic front; twin shocks rear	
Brakes Single disc front; drum rear	
Weight 542lb (246kg) wet	
Top speed 132mph (212km/h)	

Left: This bike is a 1974-model Z1-A, differing from the previous year's original model in its paint scheme and alloy (instead of black) cylinder finish.

Having created a bike of outstanding performance, Kawasaki gave it looks to match. The Z1's curved petrol tank, small sidepanels and rear duck tail combined with the big, heavily finned air-cooled powerplant to make a very handsome machine. Chassis specification was conventional. The engine was angled slightly forward in a twin-downtube steel frame whose forks held a 19-inch wheel and single brake disc. High, wide handlebars resulted in a wind-blown riding position but helped the rider manoeuvre the physically big four, which weighed a substantial 542lb (246kg).

Brutal acceleration was the Z1's most thrilling attribute. The big twin-cam motor delivered huge reserves of torque from low revs, sending the bike storming to a top speed of over 130mph (209km/h) at a rate that riders of other bikes could only dream about. It was also impressively smooth, even when running up to its 9000rpm redline. Equally importantly the big motor proved superbly reliable, even when fitted with the tuning parts soon developed by a host of eager specialists.

The Z1's chassis also benefited from attention, because the bike's blend of power, weight and relatively simple frame and suspension caused a few problems. For restrained riding the Kawasaki was well controlled and reasonably comfortable, despite its high bars. But its high-speed stability was marginal, especially under aggressive cornering. Many riders fitted a hydraulic steering damper, which helped. Others turned to custom-made chassis from specialists including Harris, Bakker, Moto Martin, Egli and Bimota.

Plenty of other owners were more than happy with the standard Z1, whose fearsome reputation added to its appeal. Such was the Z1's lead over the opposition that Kawasaki barely had to update it for several years. Eventually in 1976 a second front brake disc, previously an optional extra, was fitted as standard, and the bike was renamed the Z900.

At the same time the engine was detuned slightly, with new carbs and pipes, to reduce emissions for the US market. By then the big four was firmly established as the King of the Road, and had earned Kawasaki an enviable and lasting reputation for brutal, unburstable four-cylinder performance.

Below: When pushed hard in corners the Z1's power and weight were too much for its chassis, making fitment of a steering damper advisable.

Suzuki GT750

Above: *The GT750's size, relaxed riding position and big dual seat marked it out as a bike built more for comfort than pure speed, and the two-stroke triple motor's broad power band added to its versatility.*

The GT750 was not the most sleek and sophisticated machine in the years following its introduction in 1972. But the bulbous three-cylinder two-stroke was one of the most glamorous, and became one of the most popular early superbikes.

Suzuki's engineers created the GT around a 738cc, piston-ported two-stroke engine that was essentially one-and-a-half units from the air-cooled T500 twin. Retaining the twin's cylinder dimensions, and adding an extra cylinder plus liquid-cooling, boosted maximum output to 67bhp with a matching increase in midrange response. The chassis was conventional, with a twin-downtube frame, gaitered front forks and twin shocks.

The GT was a true Grand Tourer. Built as much for smoothness and comfort as for pure speed, it produced abundant midrange torque, had a roomy and comfortable riding position, and was a capable all-rounder that could cover large distances rapidly and with a certain style.

Its look was unmistakable. The big Suzuki's rounded shape, unusual paint schemes and bulky liquid-cooled engine earned it the nicknames of 'Water Buffalo' in the US and the 'Kettle' in the UK. As well as the smooth, water-jacketed cylinders it stood out due to its large radiator and black-tipped reverse-cone silencers.

Straight-line performance was good rather than exceptional. The Suzuki's 524lb (238kg) of weight limited acceleration towards its 110mph (177km/h) top speed. The big triple was happiest being ridden relatively gently, when its rider could appreciate its long-legged feel and ability to cruise smoothly at around the legal limit.

Chassis performance also rewarded a relatively relaxed riding style. In most situations the GT was stable, if soft and ponderous, but more aggressive cornering resulted in the frame and suspension generating some unpleasant wallowing. Braking was reasonably good, thanks mainly to the twin-sided, twin leading-shoe front drum.

Hopes that Suzuki would develop a sportier triple came to nothing, although the firm did increase the power output slightly. The GT750L of 1974 produced 70bhp thanks to modifications including extra compression ratio, CV carbs and a new exhaust system. It was slightly faster but less smooth than the earlier model.

The liquid-cooled triple's tuning potential was shown by Suzuki's racing derivative, the TR750. It produced 100bhp and was the first bike to be timed at over 170mph (274km/h) at Daytona, but earned the nickname 'Flexy-flyer' with a vicious high-speed wobble. In its improved XR11 guise the TR was later raced to many wins by Barry Sheene and others.

Chassis updates to the GT750 roadster were limited to the introduction of a twin-disc front brake, plus details including a digital gear indicator and lockable fuel cap. They were not enough to keep the two-stroke in production after 1976, when motorcycle manufacturers came under pressure from tightening emissions laws and rising oil prices.

The GT750 is long gone, but it is not forgotten thanks to the enthusiasm of owners' organisations in many countries. Suzuki has built plenty of faster and more sophisticated machines over the years, but there is something special about the charismatic two-stroke triple.

Suzuki GT750J (1972)	
Engine	Liquid-cooled two-stroke triple
Capacity	738cc (70 x 64mm)
Maximum power	67bhp @ 6500rpm
Transmission	Five-speed, chain final drive
Frame	Steel twin downtube
Suspension	Telescopic front; twin shocks rear
Brakes	Drum front & rear
Weight	524lb (238kg)
Top speed	110mph (177km/h)

Above: The softly-tuned, liquid-cooled 738cc motor produced a modest 67bhp in standard form, but the 100bhp TR750 racing triple proved its tuning potential.

Left: The big Suzuki was ideally suited to effortless open-road cruising with plenty of acceleration in hand to its 110mph (177km/h) top speed.

BMW R90S

Bmw's refined R90S was arguably the finest all-round superbike of the mid-1970s. Resplendent in its distinctive smoked grey or orange paint scheme, the R90S was the sporting flagship of a line of flat-twins that stretched back half a century to BMW's first motorcycle in 1923. Some superbike rivals were more powerful; others more agile. But none could match the refined German boxer's combination of relaxed high-speed cruising ability, fine handling, reliability and impeccable finish.

Its 898cc powerplant was a tuned version of BMW's air-cooled R90/6 unit, complete with traditional pushrod valve operation and shaft final drive. Larger Dell'Orto carburettors and increased compression ratio helped increase maximum output to 67bhp. The R90S's top speed of around 125mph (200km/h) was impressive, as were its strong and responsive midrange acceleration and its smoothness throughout the range. Equally importantly, the bike's blend of flat handlebars and stylish bikini fairing allowed relaxed high-speed cruising.

Handling was good by contemporary standards, aided by the twin's relatively light weight of 474lb (215kg) with fuel. The fairly soft suspension worked well, and the brakes, which were uprated for 1975 after initial complaints, were subsequently adequate. Useful features included a dashboard clock, plus generous fuel range and a seat that allowed the rider to make the most of it. BMW's flagship had a price that matched its high specification: in many markets it cost more than twice as much as Honda's CB750 four. But for covering long distances at speed, few superbikes came even close to matching it.

Above and below: The R90S's combination of bikini fairing and smoked paintwork gave an unmistakable look that perfectly reflected the BMW flagship's unmatched combination of build quality and all-round performance.

Benelli 750 Sei

Benelli's 750 Sei became the world's first six-cylinder superbike on its launch in 1974, and came backed by the Italian marque's four-stroke racing pedigree, which included victory in the 250cc world championship in 1969. The Sei combined its unique engine layout with high-quality chassis parts. But despite its glamorous specification, the conservatively styled Sei contained little advanced engineering. Its 748cc, sohc engine, commonly criticised as resembling one-and-a-half Honda CB500-four units, produced a modest 71bhp, which meant the Benelli lacked the performance of the best rival Italian superbikes.

The six-cylinder engine was commendably narrow. A trio of dual-manifold Dell'Orto carbs left the rider plenty of kneeroom, as well as providing crisp throttle response and plenty of midrange torque. But although the softly-tuned Sei cruised with impressive smoothness, its large frontal area contributed to relatively tame acceleration and a top speed of only 115mph (185km/h). Chassis performance was more impressive, for despite its big motor the Benelli handled well. Its strong steel frame held high-quality Marzocchi suspension. Twin Brembo front discs gave powerful braking.

Benelli had hoped that the Sei's unique engine layout would add sufficient glamour to make the bike popular. But its unexceptional performance and high price proved more relevant than its number of cylinders and the fact that it was a capable all-rounder. Despite slow sales, the Sei remained in production throughout the 1970s with few changes, before its engine was enlarged to create the more powerful – but no more successful – 900 Sei.

Benelli 750 Sei (1974)	
Engine	Air-cooled, sohc 12-valve transverse six
Capacity	748cc (56 x 50.6mm)
Maximum power	71bhp @ 8500rpm
Transmission	Five-speed, chain final drive
Frame	Steel twin cradle
Suspension	Telescopic front; twin shocks rear
Brakes	Twin discs front; drum rear
Weight	484lb (220kg)
Top speed	115mph (185km/h)

Below: The Sei had restrained styling but there was no mistaking its unique engine layout, which was enhanced by the six-pipe exhaust system. This bike is fitted with Benelli's accessory rear carrier.

Above: The Benelli did not have outstanding straight-line performance but its flexible and smooth 748cc six-cylinder motor gave effortless cruising potential.

Honda GL1000 Gold Wing

urpose-built touring bikes have evolved so much since the Honda Gold Wing's launch in 1975 that the original GL1000 seems almost inadequate for serious long-distance riding. Yet when the GL was introduced, its size, style and sophistication polarised opinions between riders in the US, where the flat-four engined Honda's smoothness and comfort were immediately recognised, and European markets where the bike's size and complexity led to heavy criticism.

The fuss in the UK bike press, in particular, seems curious in retrospect because the subject of the debate was a bike whose unfaired layout and softly-tuned 999cc engine gave little hint of the huge, fully faired and lavishly equipped machine that the Gold Wing was later to become. The GL1000 had no fairing, top-box, passenger back-rest or panniers. No sound system or cruise control, and certainly no reverse gear, as on more recent Wings.

Honda's development team had begun work in 1972. Their first prototype was a 1470cc flat six, code-named the AOK. But although the engine reportedly worked well, its length created problems. Instead, Honda's engineers opted for a flat-four engine featuring single overhead camshafts driven by toothed belts. Peak power output was 80bhp.

The Wing's chassis was relatively conventional, based around a tubular-steel frame, though it incorporated a dummy fuel tank that contained a kick-start lever and a small amount of storage space. Fuel lived under the seat, which helped lower the centre of gravity of a bike which, at 638lb (290kg) with fuel, was far heavier than contemporary superbikes.

Straight-line performance was impressive; not so much the 120mph (193km/h) top speed as the long-legged cruising ability provided by the smooth-running flat-four motor. Despite its weight, the Wing accelerated at a thrilling rate, too.

Above: The original Wing's 999cc engine sat under a dummy tank, and was fed with fuel from a tank beneath the seat. The flat-four unit was smooth, flexible and had a low centre of gravity.

Left: For such a big, heavy bike the Gold Wing handled well but it was best suited to touring on long, relatively straight roads in the US.

Its time of just under 13 seconds for the standing quarter mile put it behind only Kawasaki's Z1 in the superbike charts.

The GL1000 incorporated some notable flaws, most obviously its small under-seat fuel tank, which gave a range of less than 100 miles (161km) at speed; and the fact that the exposed riding position and hard seat made even this modest distance uncomfortable. Other problems included the uselessly pessimistic fuel gauge, which was set into the dummy tank and got in the way of a tank bag.

For such a heavy machine the Honda handled improbably well. Although it always felt like a big bike, its suspension was reasonably well controlled and the flat-four engine's low centre of gravity aided slow-speed manoeuvres. The wide bars made steering fairly light, despite the long wheelbase and 19-inch front wheel.

The GL1000's unsuitability for spirited riding was one reason for its mixed reception in Europe. But that mattered little to the older, touring-oriented US riders who rapidly adopted the smooth, quiet and refined Honda with great enthusiasm, often adding accessories ranging from fairings and luggage to extra chrome and lights. The cult of the Gold Wing had arrived, and motorcycle touring would never be quite the same – especially after 1980, when Honda added a fairing and hard luggage to the standard package.

Above: The original GL1000's simple, unfaired layout gave no hint of the luxurious, comprehensively equipped tourer that the Gold Wing would become in future years.

Honda GL1000 Gold Wing (1975)	
Engine	Liquid-cooled sohc eight-valve flat four
Capacity	999cc (72 x 61.4mm)
Maximum power	80bhp @ 7500rpm
Transmission	Five-speed, shaft final drive
Frame	Steel twin downtube
Suspension	Telescopic front; twin shocks rear
Brakes	Twin discs front; disc rear
Weight	638lb (290kg) wet
Top speed	122mph (196km/h)

Ducati 900SS

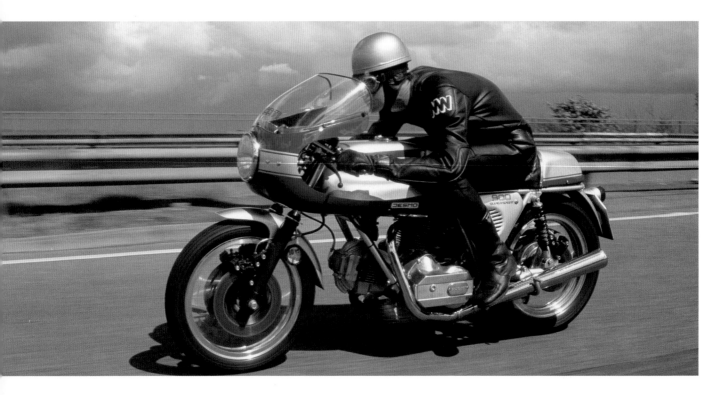

Ducati's lean, loud 900SS was proof of the beauty that could result from a motorcycle designed purely for speed. Single-minded to the point of being starkly functional, the booming Super Sport V-twin blended track heritage with a complete absence of frills. It was launched in 1975 as a development of the 750SS, a limited-edition replica produced to celebrate Paul Smart's victory in the prestigious 1972 Imola 200 race. The 750SS was so successful that the factory built more, then enlarged the engine to 864cc to create the 900SS.

Its 90-degree V-twin used bevel-gear drive to single overhead cams, plus desmodromic valve operation. Sucking in through huge, unfiltered 40mm Dell'Orto carbs and exhaling freely through Conti pipes, the 900 produced a healthy 79bhp. Notably slim and uncluttered, lacking even indicators or an electric starter, the 900SS scaled just 414lb (188kg). With its rider gripping clip-ons behind the silver and blue half fairing, the Ducati roared to over 130mph (209km/h) and cruised at high speed with an intoxicatingly smooth long-legged feel.

Equally importantly, the ultra-stable handling provided by its rigid steel frame and stiff Marzocchi suspension meant that the 900 could be held flat out through bends that forced rivals to shut-off. And when the rider did need to slow, there were no better brakes in motorcycling than the Ducati's trio of Brembo discs. The 900SS remained in production for almost a decade, although some later models were detuned. Mike Hailwood's famous 1978 TT victory inspired the following year's successful Mike Hailwood Replica version of the V-twin, featuring a full fairing in Hailwood's green and red paint scheme.

Above: Few rival superbikes could even approach the speed or riding sensation of a 900SS in full flight, with its long-legged feel and thunderous V-twin exhaust note.

Above: The Ducati's uniquely uncompromising specification included big twin front discs, a half fairing and single seat, but not such luxuries as indicators or an electric starter.

Laverda Jota

Laverda's handsome three-cylinder Jota was the most powerful and arguably the fastest of the great Italian superbikes of the 1970s. Powered by a tuned version of the Breganze firm's 981cc dohc three-cylinder engine, it was a big, brutal charger that required plenty of rider input – and rewarded it with breathtaking performance and a spine-tingling exhaust wail.

The Jota resulted from a collaboration between Laverda and Slater Brothers, its UK importer. At Slater's request, Laverda fitted its existing 3C triple with the hot cams and high-compression pistons used by factory endurance racers. Free-breathing pipes completed a 90bhp beast that stormed to a top speed of almost 140mph (225km/h). The tall, heavy triple was prone to high-speed instability but generally handled well, with the help of typically firm Ceriani suspension. Triple Brembo discs gave powerful braking. Numerous production race victories proved that with the right rider, the Jota was the world's fastest superbike.

As a roadster the Jota was demanding. Its vicious acceleration combined with the unfaired riding position, engine vibration and heavy clutch to make every journey an event. In other respects the Laverda was well equipped, with finish and electrics that were excellent by Italian standards. In 1980 Laverda added a half fairing, and in 1982 smoothed the engine by redesigning it with equal, 120-degree firing intervals, in place of the original 180-degree (two pistons up, one down) arrangement. The Jota 120 was more practical and just as fast, although some diehard Jota fans still preferred the uniquely raw and charismatic original.

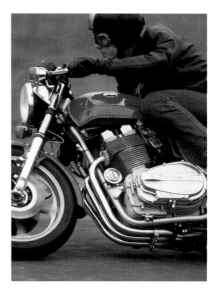

Above: The Jota demanded a forceful riding style but was capable of fast cornering, as its many production race wins confirmed.

Below: Laverda's big triple was an imposing machine whose performance very much lived up to the muscular look.

Moto Guzzi Le Mans 850

The Le Mans was arguably the most stylish and charismatic of all the great 1970s Italian superbikes. It was certainly one of the fastest. Around the unlikely basis of its transverse V-twin engine, Moto Guzzi fashioned a sports machine that backed up its quintessentially Italian look with exhilarating speed plus outstanding handling and braking. The Le Mans made a magnificent roadster and a useful production racer, and is regarded by many Moto Guzzi fans as the finest bike that the famous old firm has ever produced.

Guzzi created the Le Mans in 1976 by enlarging and tuning the 90-degree, pushrod-operated V-twin engine of the existing 750 S3 roadster – itself a rapid and handsome machine – and adding a bikini fairing, curvaceous petrol tank, uniquely sculpted seat, and paintwork in Italian racing red. Capacity rose to 844cc from the S3's 748cc, the compression ratio was raised, and the motor gained tuning parts including unfiltered Dell'Orto carburettors and free-breathing exhaust. Peak output increased from 72 to 80bhp, and midrange power was also significantly boosted through the rev range.

Straight-line performance was deliciously strong. The big motor was lumpy at low revs, but smoothed and pulled harder through the midrange. The V-twin unit's new-found top-end power gave storming acceleration to a top speed of 130mph (210km/h). Equally addictive was the Le Mans' smooth, relaxed feel which, in combination with the flyscreen's protection, slightly leant-forward riding position and well-padded seat, allowed prolonged high-speed riding in reasonable comfort.

The Le Mans was not the lightest or most agile of superbikes but it handled well, helped by a stiff steel frame and taut suspension. Many '70s superbikes of

Below left: The Le Mans' taut and well-damped suspension helped give handling that was a match for almost every rival superbike, despite its shaft final drive.

Below: With its handlebar fairing, sculpted seat and big, rounded cylinders, Guzzi's flagship had the style to complement its unique brand of high performance.

comparable performance were prone to high-speed weaves, but the V-twin was generally unshakable, and was confidence-inspiring in bends despite the occasionally distracting effect of the shaft final drive. Guzzi's unique linked brake system of three cast-iron Brembo discs was powerful and reliable, too, even in the wet. The handlebar lever operated one front disc; the foot pedal the other plus the rear. Apart from typically poor electrics, the bike was also well built and reliable.

An inevitably high price ensured that the Le Mans did not sell in vast numbers, but Guzzi's flagship boosted the firm's image and gained a strong following. The model remained in production for 19 years, through a series of generally unimpressive updates. The Le Mans Mk2 of 1979 featured an angular full fairing, but was slightly slower. The 1982-model Mk 3 regained some power, but by then the pushrod V-twin had become less competitive. Worse was to follow in 1985 with the curiously styled, 949cc Mk 4, which handled poorly thanks to a 16-inch front wheel introduced without a corresponding change in steering geometry.

The disappointment of the later Le Mans models was heightened by memories of the elegance and competitive performance of the first one. Subsequent V-twins restored some pride to the marque from Mandello del Lario, but it's debatable whether Guzzi or any other firm will build a superbike more stylish and soulful than the original Le Mans 850.

Above: *Guzzi's transverse V-twin engine had come a long way since its unlikely beginnings in the firm's tractor-like three-wheeled vehicle of the early 1960s.*

Moto Guzzi Le Mans 850 (1976)	
Engine	Air-cooled ohv four-valve pushrod 90-degree transverse V-twin
Capacity	844cc (83 x 78mm)
Maximum power	80bhp at 7300rpm
Transmission	Five-speed, shaft final drive
Frame	Steel spine
Suspension	Telescopic front; twin shocks rear
Brakes	Twin discs front; single disc rear
Weight	476lb (216kg) wet
Top speed	130mph (210km/h)

Harley-Davidson XLCR1000 Café Racer

The long, black Café Racer that Harley-Davidson launched in 1977 was the unlikeliest of superbikes. Its basic layout was promising: handlebar fairing, flat bars, big V-twin engine and rearset footrests. Some parts were borrowed from Harley's Sportster, others from the legendary XR750 dirt-tracker. But although the XLCR1000 looked mean and had an undeniable charisma, it was far from the fast, aggressive, Italian-style V-twin charger that its styling suggested.

Its air-cooled, 45-degree V-twin motor came direct from the Sportster, so was a softly-tuned 998cc unit with pushrod valve operation, four-speed gearbox and a peak output of 61bhp. The engine was mounted solidly in a frame that combined a Sportster front end with XR750 components. Forks and shocks were borrowed from the Sportster, though the Café Racer gained a second front disc brake and Goodyear tyres.

The XLCR's basic problem was that, although Harley's traditional engine and chassis technology worked well with a cruiser, it was much less suited to a bike with sporting pretensions. The big V-twin kicked out enough low-down torque to send the Café Racer thundering to 120mph (193km/h). But vibration was a problem even at much slower speeds, and cornering was severely limited by the crude suspension and poor ground clearance. At the time the bike did not appeal either to sporting riders or to Harley's traditional cruiser crowd. These days the verdict is more generous, and the XLCR's style, sound and charisma make up for the fact that it never really was a true Café Racer at all.

Above: The Café Racer's bikini fairing and big V-twin engine gave the look of a racy Italian superbike, but the Harley was a much more laid-back machine.

Above left: Cast-alloy wheels and twin front brake discs were standard fitments, and this XLCR also benefits from a fork brace that added front-end stability.

Suzuki GS1000

The GS1000 heralded a second generation of Japanese four-cylinder design on its arrival in 1978. Suzuki's first open-class superbike was more powerful and faster than any previous mass-produced four. More importantly, the GS had a strong and sophisticated chassis that not only made it the best handling big bike yet from Japan, but arguably the first whose cornering ability was comparable with that of leading European rivals.

For a machine with such stellar performance the GS1000 had an unspectacular appearance, with restrained styling, slightly raised bars and an air-cooled, 997cc twin-cam engine that resembled those of Suzuki's own GS750 (which had been launched a year earlier) and Kawasaki's Z1000. What was outstanding was the way the motor performed. The GS made 4bhp more power than the benchmark Kawaski, with a maximum of 87bhp. It also developed more torque throughout the range, and was lighter and equally reliable.

A strong, twin-downtube frame held suspension more sophisticated than anything previously seen on a mass-produced roadster. Front forks were air-assisted, and the shocks could be adjusted for rebound damping as well as for the normal preload. Powerful triple disc brakes were marred only by a slight wet-weather delay typical of the time. It added up to a stunning new superbike, as happy scorching smoothly to its 135mph (217km/h) top speed as it was cruising effortlessly or being hustled along a twisty country road. Kawasaki's Z1000, for so long the King, was deposed by a bike that was superior in virtually every respect.

Above: Visually similar to the GS750, the GS1000 combined a strengthened twin-downtube frame design with the most sophisticated suspension yet from a mass-produced four.

Above: Suzuki's 997cc, dohc engine was more powerful than and just as robust as the Kawasaki Z1000 unit that it closely resembled.

Honda CBX1000

The CBX1000 divides opinions like few bikes ever built. In many respects Honda's mighty six was an outstanding superbike. When unleashed in 1978 it was the world's most powerful production machine; a pure-bred sports bike that owed its inspiration to Honda's fabulous multi-cylinder racers of the 1960s, and whose chassis was boosted by innovative use of lightweight materials. But the expensive CBX sold poorly and was soon dropped from Honda's range.

Its heritage was certainly an inspiration for the bike's project leader Shoichiro Irimajiri, who as a young engineer in the 1960s had worked on the high-revving multi-cylinder Honda Grand Prix bikes ridden to world titles by stars including Mike Hailwood. Race-bred technology was used to design the dohc cylinder head, which held 24 tiny valves. The CBX was innovative in its use of magnesium for some engine covers, and the powerplant featured a hollow exhaust camshaft for further weight reduction.

Neat engine details included a jackshaft, above the gearbox, which drove the alternator and ignition system. This allowed the 1047cc motor to be very narrow at its base. Legroom was provided for the rider by tilting the cylinders forward by 33 degrees, and by angling the six carburettors inwards in two banks of three. Maximum output was 105bhp at 9000rpm.

Styling was dramatic, emphasised by the way in which the massively broad engine, which being air-cooled required no radiator, was suspended by the tubular-steel frame. The absence of downtubes added to the impact of a machine that was rare in being designed as a no-compromise sports machine, at a time when much of Honda's focus was on the touring-oriented US market.

Straight-line performance was majestic, combining shoulder-splitting acceleration with remarkable six-cylinder smoothness. At low revs the CBX

Above: Honda suspended the CBX engine from its frame in order to keep the dramatic bank of six air-cooled cylinders in full view, adding greatly to the bike's visual appeal.

Honda CBX1000 (1978)	
Engine	Air-cooled dohc 24-valve six
Capacity	1047cc (64.5 x 53.4mm)
Maximum power	105bhp @ 9000rpm
Transmission	Five-speed, chain final drive
Frame	Tubular-steel
Suspension	Telescopic front; twin shocks rear
Brakes	Twin discs front; disc rear
Weight	572lb (260kg) wet
Top speed	135mph (217km/h)

responded obediently and without fuss. When the rev-counter needle reached 6000rpm the bike came alive, leaping towards its 135mph (217km/h) top speed with a high-pitched howl from its exhaust.

Handling was excellent for a big machine that scaled 572lb (260kg) despite Honda's attempts to save weight by using aluminium handlebars, plastic mudguards and magnesium engine covers. Suspension was reasonably firm and well-damped, stability was good, and the bike also slowed reliably thanks to a capable twin-disc front brake.

The glamorous Six generated a storm of publicity on both sides of the Atlantic, much of it favourable. But sales were disappointing, especially in the US. Some motorcyclists were wary of its relatively untried technology, but for many the main drawback was price. The CBX was typically 50 per cent more expensive than comparable fours, yet its performance advantage was minimal.

Honda had no more joy with the fully faired CBX1000B, introduced in 1981. Aimed at touring riders, it also sold slowly. The bold six-cylinder gamble had failed but the Six had given Honda's image a much needed boost. Years later it retains a cult following, based on the unique way that it combined style, technology and performance. Few people would conclude that the CBX was a success, but the two-wheeled world would have been much less interesting without it.

Below: This immaculate CBX is fitted with the accessory engine bars that helped protect its wide engine in a crash. The high price and running costs contributed to the fast and stylish Honda's commercial failure.

Kawasaki Z1300

The arrival of Kawasaki's gigantic, controversial Z1300 six in 1979 provided a perfect final chapter for the remarkable motorcycling story of the 1970s. Superbikes had been getting bigger, more powerful, heavier and more complex throughout the decade, but there had been nothing to compare with the Z1300, which pushed the envelope in every direction. Its enormous 1286cc six-cylinder engine produced 120bhp, making it the world's most powerful streetbike by a clear 15bhp. Despite having no fairing, the Z1300 weighed 670lb (305kg) with fuel, and added the complexity of liquid-cooling and shaft final drive to its engine's dohc, 12-valve specification.

Its large radiator meant the slab-sided Kawasaki gained little visual impact from its engine layout. A massive steel frame and well-chosen suspension at least meant that it had improbably good handling to match its searing acceleration. It whistled to its 135mph (216km/h) top speed without a wobble, was stable even in fast curves, and had efficient brakes and tyres. But the bike's exposed riding position and forward-set footrests meant its rider struggled to exploit the engine's effortless high-speed ability. And although the Six was smooth, its snatchy throttle response and busy feel did not make for particularly relaxed riding.

Despite its unmatched power, size and complexity, the Kawasaki offered nothing that several smaller and simpler bikes could not provide. The expensive Z1300 sold slowly and marked the end of the Japanese manufacturer's apparent belief that bigger was better. But it gained a cult status and remained in production, with few changes, until 1989.

Above: The giant six-cylinder Kawasaki's conventional styling and a modest twin-silencer exhaust system meant that in isolation it looked almost ordinary.

Above: For such a huge bike the Z1300 went round corners surprisingly well, thanks to well-chosen geometry, a massively strong frame and suitably firm suspension.

BMW R80 G/S

BMW opened up a whole new world with the launch of the R80 G/S in 1980. By taking one of its large-capacity flat-twin engines, and using it to power an enduro-styled machine designed for use both on- and off-road, the German marque sparked a craze for big dual-purpose bikes that would expand over the next three decades, leading to rival models from many manufacturers.

The G/S initials stood for Gelände, German for off-road, and Strasse, meaning street – and the BMW was a handy performer on both. Its engine was a 797cc version of the familiar air-cooled, pushrod-operated boxer, and was notable for its coated aluminium cylinder bores and single-plate diaphragm clutch. Its 49bhp peak output gave punchy acceleration, reasonably smooth cruising and a top speed of 105mph (169km/h). Equally important was the sound handling, on rough or smooth surfaces, which resulted from the G/S's high quality suspension and relatively light weight, plus an innovative single-sided monoshock and drive shaft arrangement that allowed rapid rear wheel removal.

The stylish, rugged and versatile G/S made a fine road bike and a very capable off-roader. It became very popular, boosted by four victories in the Paris-Dakar Rally in the early 1980s. BMW responded by developing a special Paris-Dakar version of the roadster, available as a kit or complete bike, and in 1987 enlarged the engine to 980cc, creating the R100GS. Further updates would see the GS go from strength to strength, providing opportunities for two-wheeled adventure to thousands of riders in the process.

Above: Belgian star Gaston Rahier rode this heavily modified G/S to his second Paris-Dakar victory in 1985, as BMW dominated by winning four of the first seven Rallies.

Below: With its lean enduro styling and long-travel suspension the G/S was very different to BMW's previous boxer twins, and its versatility soon made it popular.

Kawasaki GPz1100

The GPz1100 arrived at high speed in 1981 to restore Kawasaki's faded reputation for red-blooded performance. Its format was very much that of a traditional big Kawasaki four, though the GPz added the refinement of fuel injection to the familiar blend of air-cooled, two-valves-per-cylinder engine and steel-framed, twin-shock chassis. With its scarlet paintwork and angular styling, it was a muscular-looking machine that weighed-in at a hefty 561lb (255kg) with fuel, and was closely related to its predecessor the Z1000H.

Kawasaki's engineers enlarged the litre-bike's engine to 1089cc, and tuned it with bigger valves, hotter cams, high-compression pistons and a lightened crankshaft. Its 108bhp maximum output gave the GPz a horsepower advantage over every rival four in 1981, though not over Kawasaki's own Z1300 six. Its chassis was based on that of the Z1000H, with larger-diameter frame tubes, revised geometry and uprated suspension including damping-adjustable shocks.

The result was not a particularly sophisticated superbike, but it was a phenomenally fast and exhilarating one. The GPz combined vicious acceleration with a top speed of 140mph (225km/h), and also had excellent low-rev throttle response. Handling was generally good for such a big naked bike, although the Kawasaki was prone to twitch when pushed really hard in bends. Its brakes were powerful, the big motor was unburstable, and the rapid red GPz did much to put Kawasaki's big fours back in the spotlight. By 1983 the GPz1100 had gained a half fairing and monoshock suspension, confirming the marque's return to form.

Above: The GPz was a striking looking machine, with angular styling, red paintwork, and a black-finished engine and exhaust system.

Below: Cornering performance was acceptable but aggressive riding revealed the limitations of the big, heavy Kawasaki's chassis.

Honda CB1100R

The magnificent CB1100R was a uniquely fast and refined machine that showed what Honda's engineers could do when designing a high-performance superbike with little regard for cost. Launched in 1981, primarily to win high-level production races including Australia's Castrol Six-Hour, the CB1100R was based on Honda's CB900F. The air-cooled, 16-valve engine was enlarged to 1062cc and uprated with modifications including increased compression ratio, plus stronger conrods and bottom end. Peak power was increased to 115bhp, the highest yet figure from a production four.

Honda also refined the CB900F's steel-framed chassis format to new levels of sophistication. The frame tubes were strengthened, and held the most advanced suspension yet seen on a streetbike: front forks with air assistance, and twin rear shocks with adjustable compression and rebound damping, plus remote fluid reservoirs to resist overheating. The equally innovative front brake incorporated twin-piston calipers and big twin discs.

The CB1100R was fitted with a half fairing and single seat, and proved every bit as fast and capable as it looked. Its engine was flexible, smooth and powerful enough for a top speed of 145mph (233km/h). Handling, braking and ground clearance were exceptional. The small numbers built were quickly sold despite costing roughly 75 per cent more than the CB900F, and the exotic 1100R justified its price by proving almost unbeatable on the track.

Above: The original, 1981-model CB1100R's half fairing and single seat were changed for a full fairing and dual-seat the following year, but the Honda kept its unbeatable blend of tuned, 1062cc four-cylinder engine, rigid steel frame and premium quality cycle parts.

Honda CB1100R (1981)	
Engine Air-cooled dohc 16-valve transverse four	
Capacity 1062cc (70 x 69mm)	
Maximum power 115bhp @ 9000rpm	
Transmission Five-speed, chain final drive	
Frame Steel twin downtube	
Suspension Telescopic front; twin shocks rear	
Brakes Twin discs front; disc rear	
Weight 518lb (235kg) dry	
Top speed 142mph (228km/h)	

Hesketh V1000

When the Hesketh V1000 was launched in 1981 it was billed by its maker, Lord Alexander Hesketh, as the superbike that would relaunch the British motorcycle industry. The V1000 combined a powerful 992cc V-twin engine with a top-class chassis, and was hand built in limited numbers to be the finest superbike money could buy. Assembled in a workshop in the grounds of Hesketh's Northamptonshire mansion, it was intended as a modern-day Vincent; a stylish, rapid and fine-handling roadburner that proved the British could still build motorcycles of the highest quality.

Hesketh was a wealthy aristocrat who had run a successful Formula One racecar team, and his handsome V1000 was undoubtedly promising. Its air-cooled, 992cc 90-degree V-twin engine, designed by four-stroke specialists Weslake, used twin cams and four valves per cylinder to produce an impressive 86bhp. The frame was a neat structure of nickel-plated steel tubing, and held high-quality components including Marzocchi suspension and Brembo disc brakes.

The V1000's performance gave some reasons for optimism. The Hesketh was reasonably fast and smooth, with a relaxed cruising feel and top speed of 120mph (193km/h). Although heavy, at 506lb (230kg), it handled and braked very well. But, as well as being noisy and unreliable, the engine leaked oil and had an unacceptably poor transmission.

Production was delayed, faults were slow to be corrected, losses mounted, and Hesketh Motorcycles went bust in May 1992. The following year Lord Alexander set up a new firm to produce a fully faired touring version of the V-twin, the Vampire, but built few bikes before abandoning motorcycles for good.

Hesketh V1000 (1981)	
Engine	Air-cooled dohc eight-valve 90-degree V-twin
Capacity	992cc (95 x 70mm)
Maximum power	86bhp at 6500rpm
Transmission	Five-speed, chain final drive
Frame	Tubular steel
Suspension	Telescopic front; twin shocks rear
Brakes	Twin discs front; single disc rear
Weight	506lb (230kg) wet
Top speed	120mph (193km/h)

Below: The V1000 was a stylish superbike whose V-twin engine layout, high-quality cycle parts and British origin drew inevitable comparisons with Vincent's Rapide of the 1950s.

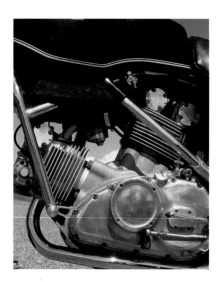

Above: Hesketh's shiny nickel-plated frame held a powerful 992cc V-twin engine, but problems of excessive noise, oil leaks, unreliability and poor transmission proved impossible to overcome.

Yamaha RD500LC

Yamaha did not hold back when, following many requests, the firm finally developed a roadgoing version of its all-conquering 500cc V4 Grand Prix bike. The RD500LC was launched in 1984, as Californian Eddie Lawson was riding Yamaha's factory OW76 to the World Championship. It was a stunning replica with a 499cc liquid-cooled two-stroke V4 powerplant, a light and well-equipped chassis, and a full fairing whose red and white paint scheme added to the GP image.

The 90bhp V4 engine was essentially a pair of RD250LC engines with cylinders set at 50 degrees, and bottom ends geared together. It shared details including bore and stroke dimensions and exhaust power valves with the race motor. The RD500LC had a frame of square-section steel tubes, though the otherwise near-identical Japanese market RZV500R followed the racebike by having an aluminium frame. Both roadster variants featured anti-dive equipped forks and a horizontal monoshock beneath the engine.

Engine performance was uniquely thrilling, with a flat feeling at low revs before the two-stroke came alive at 6000rpm with a crackling exhaust wail and a fearsome burst of acceleration towards its top speed of almost 140mph (225km/h). Handling, braking and roadholding were outstanding, thanks to the high-quality chassis and weight of just 392lb (198kg). Unfortunately for Yamaha, pre-launch excitement did not translate into sales success. That was partly due to the V4's high price, vibration and heavy fuel consumption. And partly because for roadgoing use it was simply too single-minded and racy – too much of a genuine GP replica.

Above: There was no bike to match Yamaha's V4 two-stroke for providing Grand Prix style performance, noise and excitement on the public roads of the mid-'80s.

Above: This Japanese-market RZV500R differed from the RD500LC sold elsewhere by having a slightly less powerful engine and a frame made from aluminium instead of steel.

Honda CX500 Turbo

Honda's huge and complex CX500 Turbo was like no bike seen before when it arrived in all its fully faired splendour in 1982. Previous turbocharged bikes had been specials, built for ultimate straight-line performance with little regard for cost or longevity. For the world's largest manufacturer to develop a production turbo-bike was a radical departure – and the engine that Honda chose to use made the project even more remarkable.

The basic CX500 was an unglamorous middleweight all-rounder, powered by a 497cc liquid-cooled, 80-degree transverse V-twin engine. That hardly made it ideal as a basis for turbocharging, the system of exhaust-driven forced induction that is best suited to the regular power impulses of a big, multi-cylinder engine. In fact the pushrod-operated V-twin was almost the least suitable powerplant imaginable. Cynics suggested that the bike was intended more as a statement of Honda's engineering prowess than a serious motorcycle.

The CX engine's size meant that it required the world's smallest turbocharger. Built by specialists IHI to Honda's specification, its blades measured less than two inches (5cm) in diameter and spun at 200,000rpm. Many engine components were uprated to cope. A stronger crankshaft, clutch and conrods, plus Honda's first production-specification forged pistons, helped withstand the increase in peak power output from 50bhp to the Turbo's 82bhp.

Honda put almost as much effort into the rest of the bike as into the engine, for the Turbo highlighted technology including a digital ignition and fuel-injection system, twin-piston brake calipers, TRAC anti-dive, and Pro-Link single-shock rear suspension. Its most striking feature was the fairing, complete with integral indicators and a sophisticated instrument console containing a turbo-boost gauge, clock and fuel gauge.

The fairing was outstandingly efficient, combining with the broad seat to allow high-speed cruising in comfort. But the Honda's straight-line performance was modest by superbike standards, with sluggish acceleration and a top speed of

Below left: The Turbo's comprehensive instrument panel included a boost gauge, between the main dials, as well as a fuel gauge and digital clock.

Below: The Honda's neatly shaped fairing combined with the broad dual seat to give an unmistakable look and make the Turbo a comfortable grand tourer.

125mph (201km/h). Equally disappointingly – and predictably, given its engine layout – the CX suffered from turbo lag, the delay between throttle opening and engine response that made precise control difficult.

Given the limitations presented by its engine layout, the CX500 Turbo was in many ways a fine grand tourer. It cruised at speed with a stable and long-legged feel, and handled and braked well for a bike that weighed almost 600lb (273kg) with fuel. But for all Honda's clever engineering, the bike could not fully overcome the drawbacks inherent in its complexity and weight. Its inevitably high price ensured that relatively few were sold.

A year later Honda uprated it by producing the CX650 Turbo, which was better and more exciting due to reduced turbo lag and the extra horsepower that gave arm-wrenching acceleration and a top speed of 135mph (217km/h). But even this more powerful Turbo was still no quicker than many simpler and cheaper bikes, and remained in production for only a year. The other three Japanese manufacturers each produced a short-lived turbo model before motorcycling's turbocharging revolution ran out of breath in the late 1980s.

Honda CX500 Turbo (1982)

Engine	Liquid-cooled ohv pushrod four-valve 80-degree turbocharged transverse V-twin
Capacity	497cc (78 x 52mm)
Maximum power	82bhp @ 8000rpm
Transmission	Five-speed, shaft final drive
Frame	Steel spine
Suspension	Telescopic front; single shock rear
Brakes	Twin discs front; disc rear
Weight	527lb (240kg)
Top speed	125mph (201km/h)

Above: Despite being wide enough to hide the cylinders of its transverse V-twin engine when viewed from the front, the Turbo was very aerodynamically efficient.

Kawasaki GPZ900R

The GPZ900R heralded a new era of superbike design when it stormed onto the roads in 1984. With its sleek full fairing, compact build and liquid-cooled, 16-valve engine, the Ninja was very different to the previous breed of big, air cooled, two-valves-per-cylinder fours that suddenly looked old-fashioned. The GPZ was a 908cc bike that felt like a 750 – and had the performance to outclass its 1100cc rivals.

Kawasaki's new engine incorporated a balancer shaft, cam chain at the end of the crank, and alternator above the six-speed gearbox. It was small, light and powerful, though its 113bhp peak was slightly below that of the firm's air-cooled GPz1100. The frame used the engine as a stressed member, combining steel main tubes with an alloy rear subframe. The forks incorporated anti-dive; rear suspension was a Uni-Trak monoshock with air-assistance and adjustable rebound damping. The sharply styled fairing kept most of the wind off the rider, who leant forward to near-flat bars.

Performance was a breathtaking blend of speed and refinement. The Ninja was docile and controllable at slow speed, respectably light, and most of all fast. Top speed was over 150mph (241km/h), with searing acceleration at high revs. The rigid frame, firm suspension and 16-inch front wheel gave stability with light, precise steering. Brakes were superbly powerful. The Kawasaki was also practical, combining a generous fuel range with details including luggage hooks and a grab-rail. It became hugely popular and remained little changed until 1990, when chassis updates gave it a new role as a budget sports-tourer.

Above: The GPZ900R's sharply styled full fairing helped make it faster than many naked superbikes with bigger, more powerful engines.

Below: The Ninja's 908cc liquid-cooled, 16-valve engine heralded a new generation of powerful and sophisticated Kawasaki fours.

Harley-Davidson FXST Softail

The Softail, with its new-generation Evolution V-twin engine and a classical 'hardtail' look due to hidden rear shock units, was one of the key models with which Harley-Davidson launched its dramatic revival in the mid-1980s. The comeback had begun in 1981, when the company was bought from AMF (American Machine and Foundry) by a group of senior managers. Three years later Harley introduced five models, including the new Softail, powered by a 1340cc powerplant that was superior in every way to the old Shovelhead V-twin.

Harley's new owners knew that reliability and quality control must improve dramatically if the Milwaukee marque was to compete with the Japanese manufacturers whose products had outclassed and outsold its bikes in the 1970s. A huge effort was made to ensure that the new Evolution motor, which retained the traditional air-cooled, 45-degree, pushrod-operated layout, was good enough. It produced 55bhp with a broad spread of torque, and proved lighter, cooler-running, more efficient and far more reliable than its predecessor.

The Evo unit was particularly at home in the new Softail, whose classic look, enhanced by its apparently unsuspended rear end, combined with the new engine's improved performance and durability to make the model popular. Harley reacted quickly, and two years later introduced the more retro-styled Heritage Softail plus the Softail Custom, featuring a disc rear wheel. Such was the success of these and the other Evolution models that by 1987 Harley was listed on the New York Stock Exchange, and well on the way to recovery.

Harley-Davidson FXST Softail (1984)	
Engine	Air-cooled ohv pushrod four-valve 45-degree V-twin
Capacity	1338cc (89 x 108mm)
Maximum power	55bhp @ 5500rpm
Transmission	Four-speed, chain final drive
Frame	Tubular steel
Suspension	Telescopic front; twin shocks rear
Brakes	Single disc front & rear
Weight	628lb (285kg)
Top speed	110mph (177km/h)

Below: The Softail housed Harley's sweet-running new Evolution V-twin engine in a hardtail-look chassis with hidden rear shocks, creating a bike with an appealing blend of refined performance and traditional style.

Suzuki GSX-R750

Suzuki's stunningly fast and light GSX-R750 ripped up the superbike rulebook in 1985 with a blend of race-derived design, scorching performance and uncompromising character. The GSX-R was the first true Japanese race replica; a faithful roadgoing version of Suzuki's 1000cc factory endurance machine. Its instant and lasting success inspired rival manufacturers to follow, creating the super-sports category of track-bred machines.

Race-replica bikes dated back to the 1920s and beyond, as firms including Scott, Rudge and Velocette had sold bikes based on the previous year's TT-winning machines. But the modern era had seen nothing like the GSX-R750, whose endurance-racer style twin-headlamp fairing gave a look very similar to that of the factory bike – and whose innovative, oil-cooled four-cylinder engine was held by a remarkably light and effective aluminium-framed chassis.

The 749cc engine followed its GSX750 predecessor in its dohc, 16-valve layout, but almost every component was redesigned for more power or reduced size and weight. The GSX-R employed a novel (for bikes) system of oil-cooling that dispensed with the bulk of a water jacket. Suzuki's development team, led by former race

Below: The GSX-R's styling and its format of twin-headlamp full fairing, aluminium frame and 18-inch wheels came directly from Suzuki's works endurance racebikes.

Above: *Suzuki's powerful dohc, 16-valve engine was innovative in its use of oil cooling and its emphasis on weight reduction in every area.*

Above left: *The GSX-R's light weight and good aerodynamics were as important as its 100bhp power output in generating the bike's stunning straight-line speed.*

team manager Etsuo Yokouchi, also saved weight by using magnesium instead of aluminium for the cam cover. Peak power was a highly competitive 100bhp.

Suzuki's ground-breaking use of aluminium resulted in a frame that combined cast-aluminium sections with extruded main tubes, and whose weight of 18lb (8kg) was half that of the GSX750's less rigid steel frame. Front forks were thick 41mm units, reinforced by an aluminium brace; a damping-adjustable monoshock supported the rear. At 388lb (176kg) the GSX-R was far lighter than many middleweights, let alone any 750cc rival.

There was no mistaking its uniquely aggressive intent, confirmed by low, clip-on bars and a foam-mounted instrument console whose speedometer was easily removed for racing. The bike's performance very much lived up to its image. The Suzuki was rideable at low revs but its delivery was flat until 7000rpm, when the motor suddenly came alive, howling through its four-into-one pipe as the bike surged smoothly towards a maximum of 145mph (233km/h).

The GSX-R's firm, well-controlled suspension and powerful twin-disc front brake gave it an advantage over every other bike in cornering and stopping. All was not perfect, and the original model's occasional high-speed wobble prompted Suzuki to introduce a slightly longer swing-arm in 1986. As a roadster the GSX-R was far from practical or comfortable, though its reasonably broad seat and strong pillion grab-rail were partial compensation for its narrow mirrors, high pegs and poor fuel range.

Few GSX-R750 riders were concerned about such details. The Suzuki was built for speed and it delivered, earning a cult following and inspiring a family of GSX-R fours in sizes from 250 to 1100cc. It was repeatedly updated over the next two decades, eventually gaining a liquid-cooled engine and an aluminium beam frame like many of its super-sports rivals – and throughout it all retaining the race-bred performance and aggressive image of the original, incomparable GSX-R750.

Suzuki GSX-R750 (1985)

Engine Oil-cooled dohc 16-valve four

Capacity 749cc (70 x 48.7mm)

Maximum power 100bhp @ 10,500rpm

Transmission Six-speed, chain final drive

Frame Aluminium twin downtube

Suspension Telescopic front; single shock rear

Brakes Twin discs front; disc rear

Weight 388lb (176kg) dry

Top speed 145mph (233km/h)

Yamaha V-Max

It is a remarkable achievement for a manufacturer to produce a model that will remain in its line-up for more than two decades with its look and performance almost unchanged, especially when that performance is central to the bike's appeal. That's what Yamaha managed with the V-Max, whose unique blend of street-rod styling, muscular V4 powerplant and marginal chassis created one of motorcycling's longest-running success stories.

The V-Max was designed in the US and launched in 1985. It made an immediate impact due largely to an 1198cc, dohc, 16-valve engine whose 143bhp output made it by far the world's most powerful streetbike. Yamaha had tuned the 72-degree, liquid-cooled V4 of its Venture tourer with hot cams, high compression and big valves, then added V-boost, a system that linked the carburettors to give extra high-rev power. The bike's appeal was enhanced by its dramatic, cut-down styling, highlighted by fake air scoops jutting from either side of the dummy fuel tank.

Straight-line performance was shoulder-splittingly strong. The V-Max catapulted away from a standstill leaving a black stripe on the road with its spinning back tyre, the fattest yet seen. More streamlined bikes could top the Yamaha's 140mph (225km/h) top speed, but nothing left the line or generated adrenaline quite like the V-Max. And although the near-600lb (273kg) bike's simple twin-shock chassis gave handling that was distinctly unstable at times, that merely added to its appeal. The V-Max's wild image helped it remain popular, with few updates, well into the 21st century.

Above and below: The stunningly squat and muscular V-Max look was barely modified through more than two decades of production, although ironically the Yamaha was initially detuned for many markets where its mighty 1198cc V4 engine was regarded as too powerful.

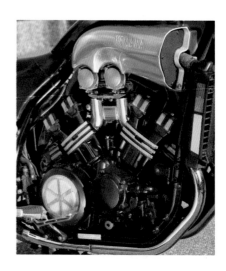

Suzuki GSX-R1100

Having rocked the superbike world with the GSX-R750 in 1985, Suzuki produced a less imaginative but even faster and more rounded follow-up a year later in the very similar shape of the GSX-R1100. As well as sharing the smaller model's endurance racer inspired twin-headlamp styling, the 1100 followed its format of oil-cooled, 16-valve engine and aluminium-framed chassis. The new bike's 1052cc motor was not only considerably more powerful, with a maximum of 125bhp, it was also notably more flexible and robust.

The GSX-R1100's frame, welded from cast and extruded aluminium sections, was a stronger version of the 750's radically light structure, and incorporated a steering damper. Identical, anti-dive equipped front forks combined with a new rear shock, wider 18-inch wheels and tyres, and bigger front brake discs. At 433lb (197kg) dry the GSX-R1100 was 45lb (20kg) heavier than its smaller sibling but remarkably light for an open-class bike.

Predictably the GSX-R1100's broad spread of power, light weight and high quality chassis made for a magnificent sports machine. The Suzuki streaked to a top speed of 155mph (249km/h) at an unprecedented rate, and provided fierce acceleration at almost any engine speed. Its brakes were powerful, and it combined precise handling with improved stability over the 750. Inevitably the racy GSX-R was not ideal for town or two-up riding, but its leant-forward riding position, tall screen and broad seat even made it respectably comfortable for high-speed blasts. And for pure performance on road or track, no other production bike even came close.

Suzuki GSX-R1100 (1986)	
Engine	Oil-cooled dohc 16-valve transverse four
Capacity	1052cc (76 x 58mm)
Maximum power	125bhp @ 8500rpm
Transmission	Five-speed, chain final drive
Frame	Aluminium twin downtube
Suspension	Telescopic front; single shock rear
Brakes	Twin discs front; disc rear
Weight	433lb (197kg)
Top speed	155mph (249km/h)

Below: The GSX-R1100's styling followed that of the 750, but the bigger machine had a stronger aluminium frame as well as the extra cylinder capacity that gave superbly flexible power delivery.

Honda RC30

The exotic RC30 that Honda unleashed in 1988 was far more than another race replica. It was remarkably close to being a street-legal version of the factory RVF750 that had dominated Formula One and endurance racing in recent seasons. Produced in relatively small numbers and bristling with high-quality components, the 749cc V4 was the most single-minded and outrageously capable roadster Honda had ever created.

Even the most authentic of previous race replicas could not compare with the RC30, which was conceived as a money-no-object basis for competition success. Officially known as the VFR750R, it followed the factory RVF to an unprecedented degree. Its compact twin-headlamp fairing and single seat unit, lightweight twin-spar aluminium frame and single-sided swing arm gave a look almost identical to that of the all-conquering works racer.

Honda's single-sided Pro-Arm had been pioneered on the innovative Elf racebikes before being fitted to the RVF endurance machines to save time on tyre-changes. Most engineers dismissed Honda's claim that it was stiffer than

Honda RC30 (1988)	
Engine	Liquid-cooled dohc 16-valve 90-degree V4
Capacity	748cc (70 x 48.6mm)
Maximum power	112bhp @ 11,000rpm
Transmission	Six-speed, chain final drive
Frame	Aluminium twin spar
Suspension	Telescopic front; single shock rear
Brakes	Twin discs front; disc rear
Weight	407lb (185kg) dry
Top speed	155mph (250km/h)

Below: The RC30 looked almost identical to the all-conquering factory RVF endurance racer, from its compact twin-headlamp fairing to the single seat and apparently unsuspended rear wheel, held by a single-sided swing-arm.

conventional swing-arms of the same weight, but the view of the RC30's apparently unsuspended rear wheel added to its appeal – and helped justify a price almost double that of Honda's VFR750F roadster.

The liquid-cooled, 90-degree V4 was a tuned and lightened version of the 750F's dohc, 16-valve unit. Peak output was 112bhp, an increase of 7bhp. The RC30 used a 360-degree crankshaft, like the RVF racers but unlike the 180-degree 750F, as this improved drive out of corners. Con rods were forged from titanium. Larger carbs, twin curved radiators and a complex single-pipe exhaust system were further RFV features.

Straight-line performance was gloriously strong, enhanced by an abundance of smooth, free-revving power from low revs. Like its factory racebike relation, the V4 accelerated in a deceptively effortless way, with a flat exhaust drone. The close-ratio gearbox's ultra-tall first ratio, good for over 80mph (130km/h), was inconvenient in town but helped keep the RC30 revving hard as it stormed towards its 155mph (250km/h) top speed.

The Honda's racetrack heritage was reflected in its ergonomics and detailing. The screen and handlebars were low; footrests high. The rev-counter and temperature gauge were foam-mounted; the speedo was separate for easy removal. The compact wheelbase and steering geometry matched the RVF's, and at 407lb (185kg) the RC30 was light by roadgoing standards.

Premium-quality cycle parts included 43mm forks and 310mm diameter front brake discs, like those of the RVF. Front and rear suspension were adjustable for compression and rebound damping, and helped give a taut and well-balanced cornering feel. The bike's breathtaking agility and braking power were complimented by impressive stability.

Honda had created the RC30 to win races, and it did not disappoint. Californian ace Fred Merkel rode a race-kitted RC30 to consecutive Superbike world titles in 1988 and '89, a feat matched by Britain's Carl Fogarty in the Formula One class. The RC30 won many other titles, too, but it's for its brilliance as a streetbike that the ultimate V4 race-replica will be most fondly remembered.

Above: The Honda's chassis rigidity, racy geometry and high-quality suspension parts combined to give superb handling, though the RC30 required careful setting-up to give of its best.

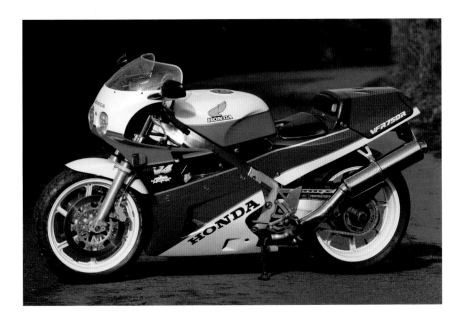

Left: Components including the rigid twin-spar aluminium frame were ready for racing with no modification, unlike the RC30's relatively heavy and restrictive standard exhaust system.

Bimota YB8

By the late 1980s the Japanese manufacturers had dramatically improved the quality of their top superbikes' chassis, but there was still scope for a small firm to create something extra special around a powerful four-cylinder engine. That was most emphatically illustrated by Bimota's YB8, whose format of aluminium beam-framed chassis and four-cylinder Yamaha powerplant followed that of the small Italian firm's 750cc YB4, which had won the Formula One World Championship in 1987.

Bimota had quickly followed its Italian factory rider Virginio Ferrari's triumph by releasing a stylish roadgoing replica, the YB4ie, that housed an FZ750 engine in a chassis almost identical to that of the racebike. The YB4ie was soon joined in Bimota's range by a similar YB6 model, powered by the 20-valve engine from Yamaha's FZR1000. When Yamaha revamped its motor and added an exhaust power valve to create the FZR1000 EXUP, Bimota adopted that unit for its own updated model, called the YB6 EXUP or, more commonly, the YB8.

The combination of Yamaha's powerful, unburstable engine and Bimota's light, lavishly equipped chassis made the YB8 arguably the ultimate super-sports bike of its day. Its free-breathing exhaust system helped the 1002cc motor produce a claimed 147bhp, with gloriously strong midrange acceleration. At just 407lb (185kg) the Bimota was 50lb (23kg) lighter than the mass-produced Yamaha, and its ultra-rigid frame, firm Marzocchi suspension and Brembo brakes gave sublime handling and stopping power. Inevitably the hand-built YB8's price was high, but it became one of Bimota's most successful-ever models.

Above: The huge, light and stiff aluminium twin-spar frame combined with the Bimota's high-class suspension parts to give brilliant handling.

Above left: The fully faired YB8's excellent aerodynamics added to the straight-line performance provided by the powerful 1002cc, 20-valve motor from Yamaha's FZR1000.

Bimota YB8 (1989)	
Engine	Liquid-cooled, dohc 20-valve transverse four
Capacity	1002cc (75.5 x 56mm)
Maximum power	147bhp @ 10,000rpm
Transmission	Six-speed, chain final drive
Frame	Aluminium twin spar
Suspension	Telescopic front; monoshock rear
Brakes	Twin discs front; disc rear
Weight	407lb (185kg) wet
Top speed	170mph (274km/h)

Honda CBR600F

There was a good reason why Honda's CBR600F was the world's best-selling motorcycle in the late 1980s. The CBR was not the most technically advanced or exciting bike the firm had ever built, but the four-cylinder middleweight provided a combination of performance, versatility, reliability and value for money that no other bike could match. The introduction of both the 600F and the similarly styled CBR1000F, which was also launched in 1987, represented a change of emphasis for Honda, back from V4s to a straight-four engine layout.

Not that the CBRs made a big feature of their liquid-cooled, dohc 16-valve powerplants, which were hidden behind rounded bodywork that provided efficient aerodynamics and reduced the expense that had to be spent on their presentation. The smaller model's 599cc engine was similar in layout to that of Kawasaki's GPZ600R, which had been launched two years earlier, and produced more power to a maximum of 85bhp. The Honda's chassis was down-to-earth, comprising a steel frame, conventional telescopic forks, Pro-Link monoshock and triple discs.

The CBR's format might not have been exceptional, but its performance certainly was – at least by middleweight standards. The refined and well-built Honda required plenty of revs for rapid acceleration, but cruised smoothly and gave plenty of entertainment as it surged to its 140mph (225km/h) top speed. Excellent handling and braking combined with the four's reasonable comfort and competitive price to make an outstanding all-rounder. The CBR600F's global popularity fully vindicated Honda's return to the straight four.

Above: The CBR's all-enveloping bodywork gave good aerodynamics and kept its 599cc liquid-cooled, 16-valve engine hidden from view.

Below: Fine handling was among the attributes that helped make the fast and competitively priced CBR600F one of the most successful bikes of recent decades.

Buell RS1200

Buell Motorcycles' production of innovative, Harley-Davidson powered streetbikes dates back to 1989 and the introduction of the RS1200. Erik Buell was a former racer and Harley engineer who had set up his own firm in a Wisconsin barn, and had used his old employer's V-twin engine to power an ingenious, fully faired racebike called the RR1000. Buell's next step was to create a roadster, the RS1200, whose half fairing highlighted the Harley connection by leaving its Sportster 1200 engine on display.

The RS1200's cut-down bodywork also revealed its high-quality chassis. The tubular-steel trellis frame held the engine via Buell's ingenious Uniplanar rubber-mounting system. Forks were Marzocchi units modified with Buell's own anti-dive system. The rear shock sat horizontally below the engine, and worked in tension rather than compression. Even the wheels and four-piston front brake calipers were Buell's work. So was the striking glass-fibre bodywork, which incorporated a seat hump that hinged to become a pillion back-rest.

Boosted by a SuperTrapp exhaust, the pushrod-operated V-twin motor produced 70bhp. It gave the RS1200 – also known as the Westwind – lively acceleration to a top speed of 120mph (193km/h), with strong low-rev response and greatly reduced vibration. The RS1200's short wheelbase, racy geometry and weight of 450lb (250kg) provided light and precise handling, too. Inevitably the Buell was expensive, costing twice as much as a standard Sportster. But it was a success, and began a line of imaginative Buell streetbikes that was expanded after Harley took over the company in the 1990s.

Above and below: The Buell's half faring left its Harley V-twin powerplant on display. It also revealed the innovative chassis with its tubular-steel frame, partial rubber-mounting system and under-slung rear shock absorber, located below the engine alongside the exhaust muffler.

BMW K1

The K1 sportster's bright, all-enveloping bodywork made it a dramatic looking machine by any standards, let alone those of traditionally conservative BMW. The German marque had decided its image needed updating, and the K1 was the result. Its ultra-slippery shape was prompted by BMW's decision to build a four-cylinder sportster governed by Germany's 100bhp power limit. When giving away 20bhp to rival superbikes in export markets, a low drag coefficient was vital.

Behind the bodywork was a tuned, 16-valve version of the K100's 987cc four-cylinder engine, featuring horizontal, liquid-cooled cylinders. A new engine-management system and increased compression boosted power by ten per cent to exactly 100bhp. The K100-based steel frame held Marzocchi forks and Brembo brakes, with optional ABS. The rear shock benefited from Paralever, BMW's system of rods that reduced the drive shaft's traditional adverse effect on handling.

For covering long distances at speed the K1 was impressive, helped by its efficient fairing, comfortable riding position and excellent fuel economy. Its engine combined a broad spread of torque with enough top-end power for a top speed approaching 150mph (241km/h). And although the BMW was long and heavy at 468lb (284kg), it had stable handling, taut suspension and powerful brakes. The K1 lacked the speed and agility of a true sportster, and for touring was marred by its frustrating inability to carry a pillion and luggage simultaneously. But the K1 was fast and capable, and succeeded in giving BMW's image a valuable boost.

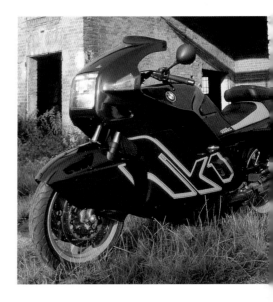

Above: The K1's large front mudguard was an integral element of its aerodynamic bodywork, helping to direct air around the bike.

Below: BMW's emphasis on a low drag coefficient resulted in a striking superbike that was very fast given its modest 100bhp maximum output.

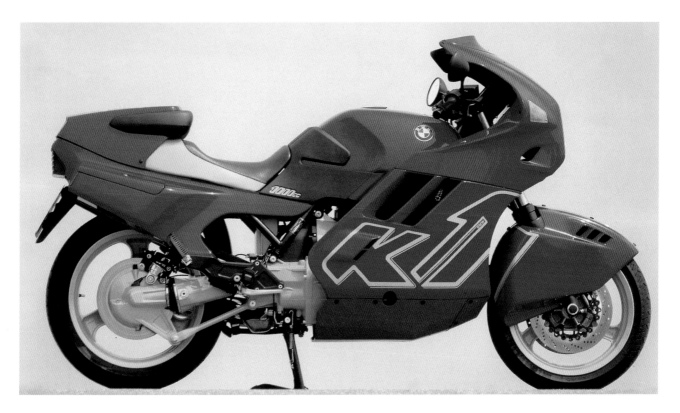

Ducati 851

The 851 was the bike with which Ducati embraced the modern age of liquid cooling and four-valves-per-cylinder technology – and came out fighting with a fast and charismatic contender. The 851cc V-twin, which retained the Bologna marque's traditional 90-degree cylinder angle, was designed by young chief engineer Massimo Bordi. His predecessor Fabio Taglioni had always rejected thoughts of an eight-valve V-twin, but Bordi pressed ahead with an engine that also employed fuel-injection instead of carburettors.

Bordi's dohc, eight-valve V-twin adapted Ducati's familiar desmodromic method of positive valve closure to give improved cylinder breathing. The result was extra midrange output and a maximum of 100bhp that made the 851 the most powerful production Ducati yet. The motor formed a stressed member of a typical tubular-

Below: The revised, 1989-model 851 handled superbly thanks to a combination of stiff frame, excellent suspension and steering geometry that suited its new 17-inch wheels.

steel ladder frame, which held Marzocchi suspension and Brembo brakes. The bike's rounded full fairing and single seat were finished in a patriotic red, white and green paint scheme.

The original 851 made a huge splash on its launch in 1988 – and received a distinctly mixed reception. Its engine was a triumph: powerful, smooth and refined, it provided thrilling top-end acceleration plus plenty of midrange torque. But the chassis was flawed. Problems of supply resulted in early 851s being fitted with 16-inch wheels, instead of the 17-inchers it had been designed for. The result was unpredictable handling, and some very confused owners.

The following year, Ducati introduced a comprehensively overhauled V-twin, finished in Italian racing red, to make the 851 the bike it should have been all along. Its engine was uprated with a modified injection system, new cams, higher compression ratio and reworked exhaust, increasing peak output to 104bhp. The frame was modified, the rear shock replaced, and most importantly the Ducati was fitted with the 17-inch wheels it had been designed to wear.

The result was a transformed bike with handsome looks, breathtaking performance, an addictive V-twin character – and handling to Ducati's traditional high standard. The sophisticated eight-valve powerplant generated vast reserves of torque from low revs to 10,000rpm. Tweaking the throttle sent the 851 thundering at a fearsome rate towards a top speed approaching 150mph (241km/h).

Better still, its taut and well-equipped chassis was now an ideal match for the engine. At 396lb (180kg) the Ducati was light, and its blend of rigid frame, high-quality suspension and now finely tuned geometry resulted in agile handling plus confidence-inspiring stability. Roadholding and ground clearance were first class, the latter enhanced by a slimmer fairing. Larger Brembo front brake discs gave even more powerful stopping.

In many markets the 851 was also reduced in price, which further enhanced its popularity, although it was still far from cheap. As well as being an outstanding roadster, it formed the basis of the snarling factory racebikes that took Raymond Roche and Doug Polen to three consecutive World Superbike titles. The eight-valve V-twin engine was then enlarged to power the restyled 916 that continued Ducati's success story through the 1990s.

Above: Ducati design chief Massimo Bordi's eight-valve, liquid-cooled desmodromic powerplant brought a new level of performance and refinement to Ducati's long-standing 90-degree V-twin engine format.

Above left: The all-red 851 of 1989 had a very different style to the previous red, white and green 'tricolore' model, introducing a refined look that Ducati's eight-valve V-twins would continue in future years.

Ducati 851 (1989)

Engine	Liquid-cooled dohc eight-valve 90-degree V-twin
Capacity	851cc (92 x 64mm)
Maximum power	104bhp @ 9000rpm
Transmission	Six-speed, chain final drive
Frame	Tubular-steel ladder
Suspension	Telescopic front; single shock rear
Brakes	Twin discs front; disc rear
Weight	396lb (180kg)
Top speed	145mph (233km/h)

Index